The Call of the Wild

A land of forest and w spectacular fusion of dee lakes and trees mingling all the reds, yellows and greens of an artist's palette… Think of Quebec, and you imagine vast tracts of virgin forest, the promised land of North America. Beyond the fringes of the cities, it isn't difficult to believe that yours must be the first human foot ever to tread on this empty and unexplored continent, that you've stepped back in time and the Far North is still waiting to be conquered. The *coureurs des bois*, 17th-century trappers who roamed this wilderness domain of the American Indians, referred to it as the "Uplands". Later, Jack London perpetuated the dream with his tales of a return to nature in all its enormity. The reality of Canada is on the same scale as its landscape: immense.

Consider the statistics; they are staggering. With nearly 10 million sq km (4 million sq miles)—600,000 of these making up Quebec alone—Canada is the second-largest country in the world, stretching 6,500 km (4,000 miles) from the Atlantic to the Pacific and covering seven time zones. It is also one of the least populated, count.
peted with forest w… easily engulf the whole of Western Europe. Quebec is six times bigger than the United Kingdom. Although no one has ever been able to count them all, it is estimated that Canada has more than a million lakes. These have proved too much to cope with, and many appear on the maps as "unnamed".

A Lesson from Nature

It's hardly surprising that the air seems cleaner here than anywhere else. In winter its purity is almost tangible: more crystalline, more penetrating than anything you could imagine. "My country isn't a country, it's winter" sings Gilles Vigneau; and indeed, for five or six months of the year, the land is exposed to occasionally terrifying *poudreries*, blizzards of snow and ice, which the Canadians dread—yet to an extent, also enjoy. Unless you experience a winter blizzard, or live through the cycle of the seasons, you will not really understand Canada. When spring finally arrives, the natural cheerfulness of the Que-

3

Reflections of days gone by in Place de la Cathédrale, Montreal.

becois blooms at the same time as the wild flowers. Every patch of grass, still brown from its long hibernation, is soon covered by hordes of citizens hungry for the first rays of the sun. The season is short and summer arrives quickly, hot, sometimes even sweltering. At the beginning of October, autumn paints the landscape with the gold and crimson blaze of the Indian summer, turning trees and tundra alike into a gorgeous canvas of colour. The Quebecois may seem to take the splendid spectacle for granted, but deep down they realize that their country has been blessed by Nature's bounty.

The Walking River

Through the province flows the great Saint Lawrence, known to the Indians as "the path that walks". It's a river unlike any other. First, it does not have a source, being an outlet of Lake Ontario. Follow it downstream: you'll find it difficult to say exactly where it ends and where the ocean begins, which is fresh water and which is salt. At low tide, you can walk along the sand bars, the banks of the river exposed by the ebbing sea, where the rocks are encrusted with shellfish. Sometimes you can see whales spouting far offshore. All along it are little islands, some

4

EASTERN CANADA

Quebec, Newfoundland
and the Maritimes

Claude Hervé-Bazin
and the staff of JPM Publications

J·P·M
PUBLICATIONS

CONTENTS

inhabited, others wild and deserted. In winter, a patrol of ice-breakers stops the river from freezing over.

The Hazards of History

Canada and Quebec, like the neighbouring United States, are cultural melting pots. You only have to make a list of the place names as you travel through the countryside: memories of French adventurers in the Monts Chic-Chocs, Bonaventure, Trois-Pistoles and Ha! Ha! Bay; Indian names retained in Mistassini, Chibougamau, Oromocto, Shawinigan; while homesick Englishmen must have dreamt of their childhood in Liverpool, London and Cambridge. The map resumes the chequered history of Canada. A theatre of endless skirmishes opposing English and French, the country suffered a lengthy period of conquests and defeats at the whims of the European monarchs, until they grew tired of warring.

The first-known European to visit Quebec was the French navigator Jacques Cartier in 1535. In 1605, Port-Royal d'Acadie was founded, and the French held possession until 1759 when Quebec was captured a few days after the Battle of the Plains of Abraham. It was finally ceded to Great Britain by the Treaty of Paris in 1763. It's something of a miracle that the French culture has survived in North America, considering that the first French settlers were shamefully neglected by the government in their fatherland. In 1759, there were only 10,000 French inhabitants in Quebec, eclipsed by more than a million English settlers further south. Louis XIV's chief minister, Colbert, gave scarcely a thought to those far-off emigrants, while Voltaire dismissed the country as "a few miserable acres of ice"—though he'd never been there to see for himself.

Canada and Canadians

The turmoils of history are still reflected in Quebec's cultural life today. From its French origins, it has gradually absorbed the adventurous spirit of the wide, open spaces. Contact with the Amerindians, the hardships of daily reality and various conflicts have forged a special identity over the generations which is not, and would not want to be, French. While they are proud to be Francophones, Quebecois like to think of themselves as a distinct society, always hitting home when it comes to linguistic conflict. It takes plenty of determination and energy for the 6 million French-speakers to hold out against 320 million North-American Anglophones. And a tenacious memory: their motto is "I remember". 5

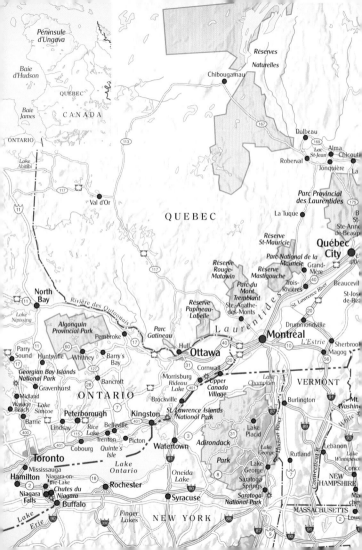

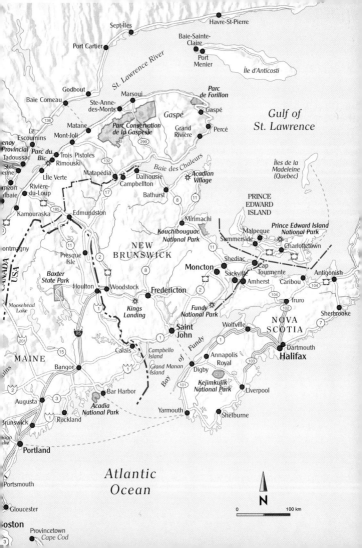

The First Peoples

Some 40,000 years ago, at the beginning of the Upper Palaeolithic era, nomadic groups from the north of Asia crossed over the Bering Strait and settled down in the greener lands they discovered in North America. Hunter-gatherers, they ventured ever further eastwards in pursuit of mammoth and bison, their preferred prey. Little is known about the way they spread across the continent. They were divided into many different nations, distinguished by language and by social organization. In eastern Canada, two groups shared the territory, the nomadic, tent-dwelling Algonquins (including the Algonquin proper, the Montagnais, the Micmac and the Cree); and the sedentary Iroquois, including the Huron and Mohawk peoples, who lived in communal houses. Much later, some 4,500 years ago, came the Inuit, who settled in the Far North. When the continent was discovered by white men, the Indians in North America numbered from 3 to 10 millions.

Nowadays, the Hurons live essentially from tourism.

European Explorers

On July 24, 1534, a storm swept Jacques Cartier, a navigator from Saint-Malo in Brittany, onto the Gaspé peninsula. He set up a cross and took possession of the territory of New France in the name of François I. When he left, he took aboard the two sons of an Iroquois chief. He was henceforth known as the "discoverer of Canada", with splendid disregard for all those who had visited these coasts before him: the Celts (9th century); the Vikings (992); various European fishermen after 1472; even the Italian navigators John Cabot, under patent from Henry VII of England (Cape Breton Island, 1497) and Verrazano (Nova Scotia, 1523). The interest of the New World for François I can be expressed in a few words: "to discover certain islands and lands where it is said that large quantities of gold and other precious materials might be found".

Further south, the Spanish had already conquered the Aztec and Inca empires, and the treasures they had looted was establishing their supremacy in Europe. By now it was known that what Christopher Columbus took to be the Indies was in fact the American continent, and Cartier imag- 9 ined he could find a northern passage to China. He reached the island of Montreal in 1535 and met a friendly welcome, but further progress westwards was hindered by rapids. Eight years later, still in quest of the legendary "kingdom of the Saguenay", he was forced to admit that Canada was not Eldorado. Meanwhile, back in France, the wars of religion put the discovery of these cold and hostile lands to the back of everyone's minds.

The First Colonies

Late starters in the race for new territories, chased out of Brazil, Florida and the Carolinas where they had attempted to settle, the French had few options. In 1584, the Marquis de la Roche tried to establish a colony, followed by Pierre Chauvin 11 years later, but neither took root. At the same time, the ships of cod fishermen and Basque and Breton whalers were becoming more and more conspicuous in Canadian waters.

In 1600, Samuel de Champlain managed to convince Henri IV to back a new expedition. He sailed along the coasts of New England, then visited New France and Acadia (Nova Scotia), where he founded Port Royal, Canada's first permanent settlement. In 1608, he undertook the most audacious of all his projects, the colonization of the banks of the Saint Lawrence. The first stones of Quebec were laid at a narrows of the river. The early days were difficult in the extreme; during the first winter, 20 of the 28 settlers died. From 1615, the first missionaries started arriving from France and buckled down to converting the pagan souls.

Champlain struggled to populate the territory and to encourage the fur trade, but the obstacles were insurmountable. The volunteers were few and badly prepared for life in the wilderness. The lands were divided into domains and redistributed to the pioneers in strips, each with river access. Settlement of Acadia did not begin until 1632.

In France, it was decreed by Cardinal Richelieu that only "Catholic Frenchmen of irreproachable character" could emigrate, thus unwittingly putting an end to any hopes of creating a populous New France. When Champlain died in 1635, only 200 hardy souls had managed to settle. Paul de Chomedey de Maisonneuve landed on the island of Montreal in 1642, at the head of an evangelical community, and began to build the fort of Ville-Marie. The population of New France had expanded to 680 inhabitants by 1651: mostly the children of poor peasants from rural France in search of a better life. A slight increase began in the 1660s.

Trading

Instigated by fishermen, fur trading with the Indians rapidly became the mainstay of New France's economy. Beaverskin suddenly became fashionable in Europe, and there was also a market for raccoon, muskrat and moose skins. Some were hunted as far away as the Great Lakes, passing from tribe to tribe until they reached the Montagnais who exchanged them for tools, arms, alcohol and cloth. In 1627, Richelieu accorded a monopoly to the *Compagnie des Cent Associés*, in return for which they committed themselves to finding 300 settlers per year. In 1664, New France became a royal province and the West India Company took over. The deal was lucrative, with profits multiplying ten or twentyfold. As the Basque merchants and Protestants from La Rochelle were forbidden to trade, they became smugglers instead. The colonists, too, wanted a part of the proceeds, and some of them took to the forest. Poor peasants, used to a life of hardship, they discovered in Canada a liberty that they'd never dreamed of. Known as *coureurs des bois*, literally wood-runners, the trappers knew nothing of royal authority and happily spent the winters in Indian camps. Children of mixed race were born of unions condemned by the missionaries.

Land of Discovery

Partly for the sake of adventure, partly for gain, the trappers penetrated ever further into the interior. In 1622, the young Etienne Brûlé reached Lake Ontario, and later Lake Erie, thus becoming the first European to see the Niagara Falls. Other explorers followed: Joliet and Marquette who descended the upper reaches of the Meschacébé (Mississippi) in 1673, succeeded by Cavelier de la Salle who discovered the mouth of the river in 1682. He took possession of the country in the name of Louis XIV and named it Louisiane in his honour. At the time, the territory was immense, unbounded to the west.

The first real journey to the west was undertaken by a certain Pierre Gauthier de Varennes de la Vérendrye in 1731. He set up several forts on the banks of Rainy Lake and Lake Winnipeg and skirted the great plains, homelands of the Sioux. His sons continued the route and discovered the Rocky Mountains.

Expansion into the interior was entirely a French enterprise: rather than consolidating their footholds on the coast, in accordance with the express desires of Paris, the explorers ceded to the temptation of new discoveries. New France was soon unable to control its vast, largely uncharted territory.

English Ambitions

Right from the start, the English colonists, Protestants, watched uneasily as the French Catholics developed a settlement right on their doorstep. Across the Atlantic, religious wars had stirred up a mutual distrust. Neighbourhood rivalries and the rallying of some of the Indian tribes envenomed European conflicts in America. In 1620, the troops of King James occupied Acadia, and in 1628 they tried to take Quebec in an effort to contain French colonial expansion. In 1670, the creation of the Hudson Bay Company diverted part of the fur trade to English merchants. To consolidate their positions, French and English built lines of forts on their respective territories.

Alliance with the Indians

Shortly after the arrival of the first settlers, attacks by the Iroquois (allies of the English) began on French settlements, hindering colonization. New France made an alliance with the Huron, traditional enemies of the Iroquois. However, smaller in numbers and decimated by imported diseases, the Huron were virtually wiped out by the second half of the 17th century. In 1689, the Iroquois massacred 320 settlers at Lachine, near Ville-Marie. In 1696, the Count of Frontenac led a vast campaign to pacify the Iroquois, which at its culmination marked the peak of French America. The following year, France recovered Newfoundland, together with part of Acadia.

British Offensive

The wheel of fortune turned in British favour after 1710. The Treaty of Utrecht of 1713 put an end to the Spanish War of Succession and ceded Hudson Bay, Newfoundland and Nova Scotia (with the exception of Cape Breton Island), to the British. The French settlers decided to stay, some of them swearing allegiance to the British Crown on condition that they would not be obliged to take up arms against their own people. In 1719, the Regent of France, Philippe of Orléans, ordered construction of the fortress of Louisburg on Cape Breton Island. For some 30 years, peace reigned and New France enjoyed a measure of prosperity.

Expulsion

The second act of the drama took place in 1754. Fighting broke out between French and British colonists (led by George Washington) in the distant Ohio Valley, foreshadowing the Seven Years War. Mistrusting the Acadian French, the governor, Charles Lawrence, decided to drive them out. On September 2, 1755 began what the French called the Grand

Dérangement, the "great disturbance". Farms were burnt down, families dispersed, many exiled to eastern America or to England, whence some of them were finally repatriated to France eight years later. In three months, 6,000 of the 16,000 Acadians were deported. Mercenaries hunted down those who had fled to the forest, where they found help from the Micmac Indians. A few found refuge on the Magdalen Islands, on Saint Pierre and Miquelon, in Louisiana, the West Indies or even South America. Years later some of them came back.

The End of New France

After several defeats, the British colonists, with the help of England, gained the upper hand over the French, who had been abandoned by Louis XV. The troops of General Montcalm, inferior in numbers, surrendered to General Wolfe's forces on September 13, 1759 after a two-month siege culminating in the battle of the Plains of Abraham in which both generals were mortally wounded. The city came into British hands. In 1763, the Treaty of Paris ceded Canada and all its dependencies (apart from Saint Pierre and Miquelon) to His Britannic Majesty, bringing to an end the war and two centuries of French history in America.

British Canada

Feeling betrayed by France, the Canadians, as they were now called to distinguish them from the British, fell back on their Catholic faith. In 1774, the Quebec Act established the Province of Quebec and guaranteed the maintenance of French civil law and customs and freedom of worship, in the hope of discouraging the population from joining the American revolutionaries. Indeed, the Quebecois were taking the side of the British. A flood of Loyalists settled in Canada. The Constitutional Act of 1791 established parliamentary government, and the territory was divided into two provinces: English-speaking Upper Canada, west of Ottawa (Ontario); and French-speaking Lower Canada (Quebec).

In 1812, war broke out between the United States and Britain, which hadn't been able to digest the loss of its colony. French Canadians fought yet again, defeating the Americans in Lower Canada. Revolutionary ideas began to inspire both French- and English-speaking Liberals, reaching a climax in the rebellion of the *Patriotes* of Lower Canada, led by Louis-Joseph Papineau. But the defeat of the rebels, supported by only a part of the population, was bitter: the Constitution was abolished and the two Canadas reunited. 13

In 1867, Quebec entered the new confederation of Canadian Provinces, together with Ontario, New Brunswick and Nova Scotia. Henceforth two Canadas developed, one French, one English. Meanwhile, the economy began to suffer with the collapse of the fur trade. City-building began, but the economic power was controlled by the predominantly English-speaking population, swelled by immigrants from Ireland and Scotland.

When French Canadians refused to fight alongside the English troops in 1914, riots broke out in Quebec. Canadian autonomy was laid down in the Statute of Westminster in 1939, but it did not prevent further conflict, and French-English disputes were revived in 1939 with British involvement in World War II. The Quebecois refused conscription, though the clergy, as usual, sided with the federal powers, and the province had to face a serious crisis. Finally obliged to join the British troops, 10,000 young Quebecois chose to desert.

The Quiet Revolution

The post-war period was marked by a period of nationalism under the sway of Conservative Maurice Duplessis, who attempted by every possible means to minimize the impact of federal decisions on Quebec.

The Liberal Party took power in 1960. Within a few years, the province was swept by a wave of revolution: a program of economic, political and educational reforms aimed at modernizing the province and intensifying its French characteristics. Censorship—one of the most retrograde in the Western world—was abolished, and education removed from the control of the clergy. Within ten years, the number of practising Catholics dropped from 80 to 20 per cent. A new separatist movement, *Rassemblement pour l'Indépendance Nationale*, was created, but things did not move quickly enough for some leaders who began to resort to terrorism. In 1963 several bombs exploded in the English-speaking districts of Montreal.

The visit of General de Gaulle in 1967 heightened the tension when he unexpectedly ended his speech with the cry, "Long live Free Quebec!"—much to the delight of the Quebecois. The following year, the election of Liberal Pierre Elliot Trudeau to the post of Prime Minister unsettled the English-speaking population. Strongly committed to improving the status of the French language,

Quebec has grown around a nucleus of stone-built houses, the Lower Town.

14

Trudeau passed legislation that included a requirement for federal civil servants to learn French. René Lévesque, a staunch separatist, founded the *Parti Québécois* (PQ) in 1970. In October 1970, shortly after the federalist Liberals under Robert Bourassa won the provincial elections, the Quebec Liberation Front kidnapped the British trade commissioner in Montreal and assassinated Bourassa's minister of labour.

In 1976, the Parti Québécois won their first victory in the provincial elections, and French was declared the only official language. On May 20, 1980, the government held the referendum proposed by the Parti Québécois on the special status of "sovereignty with economic association". But the voters rejected the plan for an autonomous state, with less than half the Francophones in favour.

A few years later, the Meech Lake Agreement attempted to reconcile the parties. Brian Mulroney, the new, bilingual Prime Minister, wanted to have Quebec written into the Constitution as a "distinct society", though the gesture was merely symbolic. But negotiations broke down yet again: the ultra-conservative anti-French regionalists of the Reform Party in the western part of the country did not want to know.

The Road to Independence?

The Parti Québécois won the legislative elections of 1994. In the eyes of the French-speaking population, however, the bicultural principle of federal Canada was in jeopardy. The antagonism of the English-speaking community, increasing immigration in the second half of the 20th century, and an extremely low birthrate in Quebec all contributed to capsizing the boat. Official bilingualism was paid lip service only.

On October 30, 1995, a referendum aiming to enact Quebec's secession failed by a whisker: 50.6 per cent voted no. With their uneasy victory, it was the winners who felt defeated. The separatists are now sailing ahead, supported by 60 per cent of the Quebecois.

What would become of Canada, were they to win? Each camp has its own answer. The English-speakers, shaken by their narrow win, have taken a tougher position. The Federalists of Quebec, in the majority around Montreal, have their own dreams of secession—"If Canada can be divided, then so can Quebec." But in fact, there is nothing to be gained by a divided Canada, with the impoverished Maritime Provinces in the east, a more prosperous west, reluctant to share its wealth, and the Francophones of the other provinces completely submerged by the Anglophones.

On the Scene

A visitor to Quebec is spoiled for choice: historic, multicultural cities stand on the threshold of the Great Outdoors; the banks of the Saint Lawrence River and the Gulf, peaceful at first, become ever wilder as the waterway nears the ocean. It's well worth venturing far from the towns, to the Gaspé Peninsula, Charlevoix, Saguenay—landmarks of Quebec's identity. And there's always the backdrop of the forest, ever more immense the further you travel north.

Canada's biculturalism has its roots in the eastern part of the country. Close neighbours, not to be missed, are the English-speaking cities of Ottawa and Toronto, and the justly celebrated Niagara Falls.

MONTREAL
Old Montreal, The Old Port, The Modern City, Mont-Royal, The Olympic Park, The Islands, Lachine, The Metropolitan Region

In 1535, Jacques Cartier happened upon Hochelaga, a large Huron settlement of 1,500 inhabitants on an island in the Saint Lawrence River. In 1608 Champlain established a trading post there, but it was left in peace until 40 years later, when Paul de Chomedey de Maisonneve founded the mission station of Ville-Marie de Montréal, in order to convert the Indians to Christianity. A few wooden houses were built around a chapel and a store, all enclosed by a stockade. At that time, Ville-Marie, future Montreal, boasted 70 inhabitants. The choice of site proved to be judicious: at the confluence of the Saint Lawrence, the Outaouais and Richelieu rivers, the hamlet became the hub of river traffic to and from the Uplands, realm of the beaver.

In 1992, Montreal's 3 million inhabitants celebrated the city's 350th anniversary. Its streets, as in many a modern American metropolis, run straight as a die, with

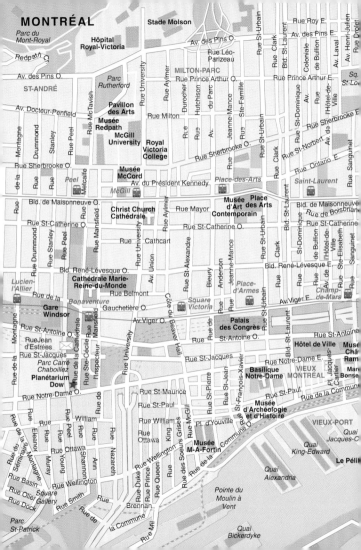

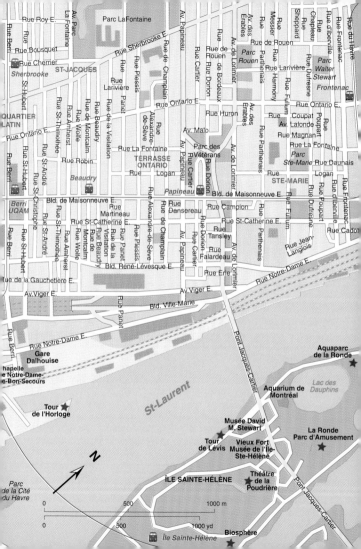

buildings of glass and steel shackled to the right-angle, the dollar and the deal. But that's only the façade, for Montreal is also the second-largest French-speaking city in the world, and knows how to relax in true Mediterranean fashion. A great melting pot of styles, the city has spread haphazardly, incorporating hamlets which form the basis of today's French, English, Italian and Chinese quarters. In spring, when the last puddles of slush disappear with the first rays of sunshine, Montreal gives itself a good shake and emerges from its winter sleep. Café owners set out their tables on the sidewalk in Rue Saint-Denis. Late in the evening, when the theatres close their doors, crowds spill out into the streets and tarry a while before turning in: Montrealers are night owls, and you might even hear them boasting of their night-time traffic jams.

Old Montreal

From the steeple of Notre-Dame de Bonsecours, you can look down on one side over the Saint Lawrence, flowing peacefully through the city, while on the other you see the place where it all began. On a small area of scarcely 40 ha (100 acres) huddles a concentration of well-to-do slate-roofed stone houses, flower-bedecked squares and cobbled streets patrolled by horse-drawn carriages. Neglected for many years, Old Montreal has been restored to become one of the jewels in the city's crown. It's worlds away from the big-city bustle of the town centre, just around the corner. Relax on the terrace of the Cartier house, lunch in one of the many restaurants, linger a while at the windows of craft shops and fashion boutiques.

Place Jacques-Cartier

Very little remains of the settlement's early days. The oldest buildings are to be found near Place Jacques-Cartier, a strip of green sloping down to the Saint Lawrence, surrounded by steep-roofed stone houses. In summer, amateur painters and street entertainers vie to attract customers. Scents from the flower market waft over the terraces of the sidewalk cafés. Slightly set back, the town hall (Hôtel de Ville) is a solid building in Second Empire style, with a green copper roof. Opposite, Château Ramezay is a stately manor house used in turn by the French governors, the West India Company, the British governors and finally the American generals who occupied the city in 1775. Today, the château is a small museum showcasing the history and culture of Old Montreal, describing the life of the colonists and displaying objects that belonged to the 18th-century aristocracy.

Closer to the river, Rue Saint-Paul is one of the best-preserved streets in the old town. On the corner stands the Calvet House, a bourgeois dwelling of 1775

NAVIGATING THE ST LAWRENCE

In North America, the port of Montreal comes second only to New York. Between Lake Ontario and Montreal, five rapids in succession lower the level of the river by 69 m (226 ft). Conceived in the 17th century, construction of the Lachine Canal in 1825 finally allowed river traffic to bypass the rapids which had confounded so many ambitious plans. In 1959, the United States and Canada together inaugurated the Saint Lawrence Seaway, allowing transatlantic shipping direct access to Lake Superior, more than 3,700 km (2,300 miles) from the ocean. A total of 17 locks (with gates that can be heated in winter) enable Quebec's pilots to guide monster vessels from the river mouth as far as the Great Lakes. Five ice-breakers keep the route open all year round for the 6,500 cargo ships which ply these waters.

---

restored and furnished with the collections of the Fine Arts Museum. Opposite, the chapel of Notre-Dame-de-Bonsecours contains a museum of costumed dolls. See also, at nos. 445 and 440 Rue Bonsecours, the Dumas and Papineau residences.

Place d'Armes

Rue Notre-Dame, lined with buildings with arched windows, leads to the most imposing sector of the old district. In Place d'Armes, you will discover Montreal's roots: the Seminary of Saint Sulpice, the oldest building in town (1685), next to the neo-Gothic cathedral of Notre Dame, obviously inspired by its namesake in Paris. The exterior is rather sober, in strong contrast with the polychrome choir in blue and gold. The stained-glass windows merit close inspection, as they relate the beginnings of Ville-Marie.

In front of the cathedral is a monument to Paul de Chomedey de Maisonneuve, founder of Montreal. The pink sandstone building turning its back to him may look commonplace; in fact it has the distinction of being Canada's first skyscraper (1817).

Place d'Youville

To the west, this square used to be the heart of old Ville-Marie. It was named after the founder of 21

"Illuminated Crowd" on Rue Sainte-Catherine: looking to the future?

the Grey Sisters Hospital (Hôpital des Sœurs Grises), a handsome 17th-century building. The old-fashioned fire station, decked out with towers from which the firehoses were hung out to dry, has been converted into a History Centre.

In the nearby Museum of Archaeology and History, you can see excavations of the earliest dwellings. The Youville stables have peaceful gardens.

The Old Port

Since 1964, the coast guards' icebreakers have kept the Saint Lawrence open to navigation all through the winter. Before then, everything used to come to a halt for four long months. In 1974, the increase in river traffic obliged the old port of Montreal to give way to newer installations further east. Ten years later, a huge rehabilitation project began and the site of the old port, cleaned and remodelled, is now the only river access available to the citizens of Montreal. Ferries tie up all along the quay. Close to the restored Clock Tower is a favourite area for walking and cycling in summer. A cinema with a giant IMAX screen attracts the crowds, as do the exhibitions and entertainment. Pleasure boats offer river cruises.

The Modern City

Montreal shows a different side to its personality once you get away from the river. Its heart is a giant rectangular grid of streets and a jungle of towers, cut through by its main street, the Boulevard Saint-Laurent. Leaving the old town, you have to pass by the horrendous Ville-Marie motorway. Behind, the dwindling Chinese district has gained little benefit from the renovations and improvements undertaken for the 350th anniversary. As in all the big cities of North America, Quebec's metropolis is being deserted for the suburbs: a dynamic policy of urbanization is intended to redress the situation.

City Centre

Place Ville-Marie is a monumental achievement of modern architecture, designed in 1959 by Ieoh Ming Peï, who later become renowned worldwide as the architect of the glass pyramid in the Louvre in Paris. Framed by skyscrapers, the esplanade is just the tip of an iceberg: below it spreads the subterranean city. In the prolongation of Boulevard René-Lévesque, the cathedral of Marie-Reine-du-Monde is a one-third scale reproduction of Saint Peter's in Rome.

Close at hand "la Catherine" (Rue Sainte-Catherine) holds the city's large stores. This is the place to go shopping in an atmosphere approaching that of the Parisian boulevards. A large sculpted group draws the throngs: English sculptor Raymond Masson's gleaming *Illuminated Crowd*.

In Place de la Cathédrale, the sparkling building of the Maison des Coopérants forms a backdrop to the small Christ Church and its triple Gothic portico.

Going back to the east along "la Catherine" you reach Place des Arts, Montreal's temple to culture, housing theatres, concert halls and cinemas next to the Museum of Contemporary Art, which is chiefly dedicated to Canadian artists and sculptural works, well displayed in attractive exhibition halls. Beyond here, Rue Sainte-Catherine becomes rather tawdry.

The Museums

Keeping your back to the river, you come to Sherbrooke Street, a sort of Bond Street with some handsome Victorian houses. This is where you'll find the big hotels, smartest art galleries and the most stylish shops. There are also several museums. Maybe you didn't come all the way to Canada to visit a museum dedicated to hockey (but who knows?). However, it is certainly worth spending a few hours in the Fine Arts Museum, at no. 1379. In a colon- 23 naded 19th-century building, a fine permanent collection traces the history of mankind from antiquity until modern times. Temporary exhibitions of high quality (Michelangelo, Dali, Magritte, etc.) are also presented here.

At no. 690, the McCord Museum of Canadian History recounts the history of Canada's pioneers, chiefly through a wonderful collection of photographs from the 1900s. Across the street, McGill University, founded in 1829, was the first in Quebec; lectures are given in English. In its Redpath Museum of Natural History, you can inspect Egyptian antiquities, stuffed animals and dinosaurs.

In Rue Baile to the southwest, the Centre for Canadian Architecture is a reputed museum, and you may also enjoy the Dow Planetarium in Rue Saint-Jacques Ouest.

Subterranean Montreal

During Montreal's freezing winters, when the blizzards blow, the people are not particularly keen on wandering around the streets. When the metro was built at the beginning of the 1970s, they started setting up shops in the stations. Then passageways were made between one building and the next. Little by little, a whole underground city developed. Today, almost 30 km (19 miles) of galleries, adjoining nine metro and two mainline stations, burrow below the ground, all accessible from Place Ville-Marie. Half a million citizens can scuttle around, go to work and do their shopping without having to put a foot outside during the cold weather from November to April. At last count, there were 1,700 shops, 200 restaurants, 45 banks, 34 cinemas and theatres and even two universities below street level.

Mont-Royal

Cartier named this hill Mont Réal in 1535. Overlooking the skyscrapers of the centre, the "Mountain", as it is called here, is an inseparable part of Montreal life. In summer families come for fresh air and picnics, in autumn they jog through the woods and startle the squirrels; in winter the frozen Beaver Lake becomes a skating rink for everyone from toddlers to granddad. And, of course, this is where the whole city turns out for its first glimpse of spring.

In the 19th century, industrial magnates built themselves magnificent mansions in stone on Mont-Royal's slopes. At the time, the 25,000 inhabitants of this area owned almost 70 per cent of all Canada's wealth, though now there's little to show for it. Nevertheless, the area is still known as the "golden square mile".

Westmount

Further west, Westmount has remained a genteel English suburb since the 19th century. Saint Joseph's Oratory, a modern cathedral, houses a relic of Brother André, a healer priest beatified in 1982. At his death in 1937, the chapel became a place of pilgrimage. Every day, believers climb the hill on their knees, following the Way of the Cross.

To the north, Outremont is another smart address, this one for French-speakers.

The Plateau

On the other side of the "Mountain", Mont-Royal Plateau is the fashionable part of the city. This is where you see those famous red-brick houses with exterior spiral staircases. The streets are lined with pavement cafés and restaurants. Frequented by artists, intellectuals and students—the University of Quebec at Montreal (UQAM) is just round the corner—it has become known as the Latin Quarter. Every summer, Rue Saint-Denis is the setting for the international festival of humour, "Juste pour rire" (Just for Laughs), when 500 comedians present over 300 shows, in theatres and out on the street. They take their sense of humour so seriously they have made a museum of it (Musée du Rire, 2111 Boulevard Saint-Laurent).

The Olympic Park

Montreal still remembers the good old days of the 1976 summer Olympic Games. Built for the event, the mammoth stadium with retractable roof is now used for rock concerts and the baseball matches of the Expos (the Montreal team). A funicular elevator hauls you to the top of the Olympic tower, a sort of inclined mast 175 m (574 ft) high, from where the view stretches 80 km (50 miles) on a clear day.

The nearby Château Dufresne (4040 Sherbrooke Street), built at the beginning of the 20th century and modelled on the Petit Trianon at Versailles, houses the Museum of Decorative Arts. Several rooms are furnished in 18th-century style.

The Biodome

The Olympic velodrome has been converted into a new type of museum grouping, under the same roof, a tropical jungle, the Laurentian forest, the Saint Lawrence Marine and a chunk of polar region. These four biotopes represent the climatic regions of the American continent. Before you enter the jungle, the ecosphere offers an introduction to the different ecosystems. In all, 350 species of plant and 250 animal species flourish in the Biodome.

The most impressive section is the Amazon, where the humidity 25 is kept at 75 per cent and the temperature is close to 28°C (82°F). Caymans, monkeys, pink spoonbills and red ibis roam around among the creepers. Past the airlock, the temperature drops and you enter the realm of the beaver, otter and lynx. Take your time or you might miss them, as they are quite shy and hide away under the trees. Working to a rhythm of artificial seasons, the biotope respects the need of some animals to hibernate. If the beavers are sleeping, you can still watch them snoring in their lodge, thanks to a hidden camera. In autumn, you can see the leaves turning red. After the next airlock, the Saint Lawrence and its immense basin, complete with screeching gannets and aquatic life, are explained in minute detail. At the Pole, snow falls from the ceiling, while Emperor and rock-hopper penguins inspect you as you pass by.

A fantastic technical achievement, the Biodome involves a great deal of maintenance. Apart from taking care of the animals, the technicians constantly monitor 4 million litres (a million gallons) of fresh and salt water, as well as the air supply of 120,000 litres per second. The Biodome is also a centre for ecological research and training, with exhibitions and displays at what is called the "the environment crossroads". The Naturalia display is intended to initiate children in the protection of the environment.

Botanical Gardens

Montreal's immense flower garden was created in 1931 and extends over 73 ha (180 acres), containing almost 30,000 plant species. A dozen greenhouses and thirty gardens are organized by theme. The Arboretum covers more than half the area. Landscape gardeners from Japan designed the stunning, deceptively simple Japanese Garden. One of the most recent additions, the Chinese Garden, is the largest of its type outside Asia and presents sixteen different landscapes. Seven wooden pavilions recreate the atmosphere of the great Ming gardens by the Yangtse. Do not miss the *penjing* collection: similar to bonsais, they are, literally, "landscapes in pots".

In the Insectarium, which looks like a giant bug, you can admire 250,000 specimens of all sizes—some are alive and crawling. The exhibition aims to improve understanding of the primordial rôle of insects in maintaining biological balance. On the ground floor, an interesting display is devoted to the somewhat unusual diet of certain peoples… and every February, the museum organizes a banquet for members of the Society of Insect-Eaters. A mouthwatering menu includes such tasty delights as grilled grasshopper, caterpillars in spicy sauce, and so on.

The Islands

Ever since the Universal Exhibition of 1967, Ile Sainte-Hélène has been home to La Ronde amusement park, with its open spaces, roundabouts and Aquapark.

In summer there is boating, in winter, skating. The David M. Stewart Museum, housed in the Old Fort, is devoted to the military history of colonial Canada (weapons, uniforms, maps, etc.). Every summer afternoon from Wednesday to Sunday, the Fraser Highlanders, kitted out in their splendid 18th-century Scottish uniforms, parade in the grounds.

Neighbouring Ile Notre-Dame was created from scratch in 1967 for the same Universal Exhibition. This is where the Montreal Formula One Grand Prix is held. You can drive round the circuit in your own car, but for you the speed is limited to 40 kph (25 mph). In building a new island from nothing, the engineers thought they might as well create a beach as well. The water is filtered through an artificial marsh, and the sandy stretch attracts 7,000 bathers per day in summer. You can hire a sailboard or a small boat.

Further west, in the heart of the Montreal archipelago, discover how millers lived and worked in the old days, in Pointe-de-Moulin Park on Ile Perrot.

Lachine

This suburb of Montreal, downstream of the Saint Lawrence Rapids, was the starting point for many of the territory's explorers. It owes its name to Cavelier de la Salle: so obsessed was he with the desire to discover a northwest passage to Asia, that his contemporaries nicknamed him La Chine (China). The Lachine Canal was opened many years later, in 1825, bypassing the rapids. The local museum (in a house dating from 1669) and the Interpretive Centre devoted to the fur trade recall the days when a handful of men made Canada's history. You can get there by boat in summer; regular excursions leave from Victoria Quay.

The Metropolitan Region

The glaciers of the Quaternary Period left behind the thousands of lakes and rivers which now thread the mountains on the city's doorstep. The citizens of Montreal, all trappers at heart, seize every opportunity to go out and enjoy this gift of nature. In spring, everyone meets up in the maple groves for "sugaring off" (tapping the maple trees).

The Laurentians

The Laurentians (Laurentides in French) is the name for the immense region of lakes and high wooded hills which stretches north from the Saint Lawrence. You will hear people speak of the Montreal Laurentians or the Quebec Laurentians. The first are the most popular and hold the greatest concentration of holiday resorts in the nation. Once you leave the motorway, minor roads lead to Saint-Sauveur-des-Monts, Sainte-Adèle, Val David, all delightful mountain villages and favourite tourist attractions. They are the ultimate family destination, with skiing in the winter, shopping in the summer, and cafés all year round.

Lanaudière

Contiguous with the Laurentians, this region is also principally recreational. The resort of Saint-Donat on the shores of Lake Archambault marks the entrance to Mont Tremblant Provincial Park. With its many rivers and waterfalls, it is a delight for lovers of forest landscapes. Closer to the Saint Lawrence and more rural, you will see the Monte-à-Peine and Dalles Falls at Saint-Jean-de-Matha, the Black River at Saint-Zénon and Lake Maskinonge. At the end of the road, Saint-Michel-des-Saints is the trappers' capital.

La Montérégie

This region close to Montreal demonstrates its cultural riches with a number of festivals. The beautiful winding Richelieu Valley, a natural route towards New York State, has played a primordial rôle in exchanges and invasions. It is the birthplace of the *Patriotes* and has kept its distinct character: historic houses and old churches in the villages of Saint-Ours, Saint-Denis and Saint-Charles perpetuate memories of the first rebellion of French-speakers in 1837.

THE BEST FESTIVAL In the middle of February, **Carnival** provides the Quebecois with a splendid opportunity to celebrate the joys of winter. For ten days ice hockey is king of all sports. Pageants are held; people mush around the streets on dog sleds; canoes are raced on the frozen river; sculptors carve the snow into incredible tableaux, ice castles and statues, destined to melt away with the thaw.

THE WEST

Hard against Ontario and touching Hudson Bay, Outaouais and Abitibi mark Quebec's last frontier. The territory is immense, scattered with lakes, rivers, waterfalls and rapids. Only a few lonely roads lead into the interior of this untamed land which has for centuries been the undisputed domain of lumberjacks and gold prospectors.

Outaouais

With 20,000 lakes and one of the most beautiful forests of the entire province, the region of Outaouais flaunts its splendours during the Indian summer. The huge nature reserve of Gatineau, on Ottawa's doorstep, is a favourite excursion for inhabitants of the capital. There are facilities for all manner of sports. The banks of Lake Meach include some lovely beaches. You can visit the estate of W. Mackenzie King, once Federal Prime Minister, a town house typical of the turn of the century.

Further north, hike around the Kenauk and Papineau-Labelle reserves, or the colossal Verendrye Reserve at the frontier with Abitibi. In winter, the region is a particular favourite for snowmobile outings.

The Outaouais River

Picturesque villages cluster along the banks of this waterway at regular intervals. The famous castle at Montebello is in fact a vast wooden structure of rounded shape. Close by, the manor house in Normandy style of Louis-Joseph Papineau, leader of the French rebellion of 1837, has

---

THE AILING FOREST

The principal industry of Quebec is lumber. Its 60 paper pulp factories employ about 10 per cent of the population and produce more than 10 million tons of newsprint every year. However, all is not well with Quebec's forests. Suffering from overexploitation and from acid rain blown by the prevailing winds from the United States, they are no longer able to keep up the supply to industry. Canada is obliged to import wood to maintain its place as leading paper manufacturer in the world. In an attempt to remedy the situation the authorities have, since 1995, forbidden the practice of floating logs down the rivers. The decomposition of the bark released too much tannin into the waters.

become as hallowed as a place of pilgrimage. The village of Oka, 60 km (37 miles) west of Montreal, is a resort which has been popular for generations. Its Trappist monastery produces a good cheese.

Abitibi

The region of Abitibi-Timiskaming, to give its full name, was for long years synonymous with exile. In the 1930s, during the Depression, the government occupied many of the big cities' unemployed by sending them off to explore these distant tracts of land. More than 60 years later, the immense Abitibi-Timiskaming is yet to be conquered. Prospectors, lumberjacks and trappers perpetuate a lifestyle handed down through four centuries of adventurers. Gold, discovered in 1908, is still mined in the Val d'Or region. There's a mining museum at Malartic.

Cœur du Québec

From Montreal to Quebec, the route follows the old "King's Road" *(Chemin du Roi)*. This is where colonization began. A few of the better houses of the first settlers still survive, in a multitude of styles that recall the

Painters and poets alike are inspired by the autumn colours.

colonists' regional origins. Sometimes the river is referred to as the high street, since 40 per cent of the province's population lives squeezed along the banks of the province's "lung".

Trois-Rivières

The first trading post in French Canada, Trois-Rivières is ideally situated at the mouth of the Saint-Maurice River at its confluence

---

INDIAN SUMMER

The Quaker colonists of Pennsylvania invented the name: at the end of the summer, the Amerindians took advantage of the last sunny days to finish their harvest. In the forests of Quebec and Ontario, it's the time when the colours burst into flame. The leaves are ablaze with every shade of gold, vermilion, purple and copper. Generous rainfall during the summer is a promise of more intensive colours. Contrary to popular opinion, it is not the fall in temperature that makes the leaves turn from green to gold, but the shorter period of daylight, which reduces photosynthesis. As the chlorophyll levels decrease, the other pigments of the leaves are revealed: carotene and xantophile, the scarlet of maple and red oak, the yellow of beech and birch.

with the Saint Lawrence. Branching round two islands, the Saint-Maurice forms the "three rivers" of the town's name. The trappers used to follow the river upstream to enter Attikamek territory, gateway to the Uplands.

One of the world's principal centres for newsprint, the town retains few traces of its past. A fire at the beginning of the 20th century spared a handful of randomly scattered old dwellings in the centre, among them the 18th-century manor of Tonnancour; the manor of Niverville (now the tourist office) and the Ursuline monastery, founded in 1697 and still in operation. Its museum displays a motley collection of furniture, ceramics, etc. There is also an exhibition centre in the Waterfront Park dedicated to the pulp and paper industry.

A succession of delightful villages dot the banks of the Saint Lawrence as it continues towards Quebec: the pilgrimage site of Cap-de-la-Madeleine; Batiscan, with its presbytery museum; Deschambault and its church; La Chevrotière and its 18th-century mill; Cap Santé, which has retained many 18th- and 19th-century buildings.

La Mauricie

At Grandes-Piles, you can gain insight into the lives of the inhabitants of the Saint Maurice valley

---

QUEBEC WINES

Planted only a decade or so ago, Quebec's vines are shared among some fifteen vineyards mainly situated in the Dunham area. Despite the rigorous climate, they produce white, rosé and red wines. The Magog wine festival at the end of September includes visits to some of the vineyards and a chance to take part in tasting sessions.

---

in the reconstructed camp complete with sawing sheds, workshops, kitchens, and so on. Retired loggers guide you around this living museum and describe the old life in the depths of the forest. There's a wonderful view over the valley from the village. The Mauricie National Park has 150 lakes and ponds, and provides forest trails, excursions by Indian canoe and skiing in the winter. Further north near La Tuque, the Blanc Reservoir marks the edge of Attikamek territory. If you organize this in advance, you can camp in the forest with Amerindian guides.

The Eastern Townships

East of Montreal, the region of the Eastern Townships (Estrie) is a combination of woods, lakes and hills in a lush countryside reminiscent of New England. After the American War of Independence, 15,000 Loyalists came to settle here in order to remain true to the Crown. You will probably notice a few of the round barns they built—so that the Devil could not hide in the corners. The "Cradle War", won here by the French colonists, somewhat reversed the trend and although the Eastern Townships are close to the American border, the language spoken is French.

Lake Memphrémagog

The biggest lake in the region is some 50 km (30 miles) long and stretches into Vermont in the USA. A chairlift carries you to the top of Mount Orford in the provincial park of the same name for a view of Magog and the entire lake. On the west bank, the Abbey of Saint-Benoît-du-Lac is a community of some 60 Benedictine monks. You can attend some of the services featuring the Gregorian chant, or, if your tastes are more gastronomical than musical, buy cheese and cider made by the monks. Opposite Saint-Benoît, the village of Georgeville has preserved its old-world charm. West by Route 245, Knowlton, on the banks of Lake Brome, is a lovely town with a Puritan atmosphere.

Lake Massawippi

Just east of Magog, this small lake is one of the most beautiful in the region. During the 1930s, rich Americans built splendid houses here, some of which have been converted into charming hotels. The hamlet of North Hatley has become a centre for many Quebecois artists.

Sherbrooke, to the north, is the "capital" of the Eastern Townships, with an old Museum of Natural Sciences and a Fine Arts Museum with a focus on local artists. The village of Cookshire, 20-odd km (12 miles) away has one of Quebec's oldest covered bridges, built in 1837.

2 THE MOST BEAUTIFUL AUTUMN COLOURS Everywhere in Quebec, when summer gives way to autumn, a riot of colours lights up the deciduous forests. According to the Quebecois, **Gatineau Park** near Ottawa is the best place of all to admire the display. However, rather further away, in the **Matapédia Valley** on the Gaspé Peninsula, the Indian summer reaches breathtaking heights.

QUEBEC CITY – MIDTOWN

QUEBEC CITY

The Old Town, The King's Road, Ile d'Orléans,
Huron Country, The Laurentians, La Beauce

In the language of the Hurons,
Kebek means "the place where
the river narrows". Built on a
neck of the river, the village of
Stadacone housed a thousand
Amerindians when Cartier landed
here in 1535. Champlain chose a
site at the foot of the cliff to build
his *Habitation* (a fortified residence) and in 1608 undertook the
construction around it of what
was to become the capital of
French Canada. "Nothing has
ever seemed to me so beautiful
and so magnificent as the site of
Quebec" declared the governor
Frontenac in 1672, writing home
to France. However, the early
days of this watchtower of the
Saint Lawrence were slow and
difficult. At this time, there were
a scant thousand inhabitants.
When Admiral Montcalm surrendered in 1759, the British entered
a town with a population 6,000-
strong.

Very different from Montreal,
Quebec takes pride in its "old
France" architecture. Built on a
human scale, its stone houses rec-
ollecting those of Saint-Malo in
Brittany, the city with its cobbled
streets, winding staircases, ramparts and the extravagant silhou-
ette of Château Frontenac has
become the leading tourist desti-

nation in the *Belle Province*. In
1985, UNESCO declared the city
to be a World Heritage site.

The Old Town

The walled town of Quebec is
perched on a promontory high
above the Saint Lawrence. On the
clifftop, the Upper Town (Haute
Ville) and its figurehead, the
Château Frontenac, are visible for
miles around, the very image of a
historic town. At the foot of the
cliffs, the Lower Town (Basse
Ville) lies by the river, a tangle of
lanes and houses with vividly
coloured roofs.

The Lower Town

The birthplace of Quebec was
around Place Royale. Although
Champlain's *Habitation* and his
trading post have disappeared,
fine stone houses recall the days
when colonists from Saint-Malo
and La Rochelle disembarked
here. If you visit in the low season, when the streets are quiet
and the summer festival is only a
memory, you can retrieve something of the atmosphere of the old
port of Quebec. The principal
building is the church of Notre-
Dame-des-Victoires, built in the
17th century and named in honour of the victories of 1690 and

1711 when the French successfully turned back English assaults on the settlement.

The Petit-Champlain quarter has the oldest alleys and the most typical buildings, including the Lambert-Dumont house (1689) in Place Royale, the Jean-Millot house (1691) at the intersection of Rues du Porche and Notre-Dame, the Leber-Amiot house (1765) at 662 Rue Saint-Pierre, and the Fornel house (1724–35) on the same street at nos. 21–25. These are the best-preserved, but many others deserve a look. Stroll along Rue Saint-Paul, under the ramparts, the haunt of Quebec's antique dealers. Rue Petit-Champlain, the smartest of all, boasts the theatre where the famous Quebecois cabaret singers perform. At no. 16, the Louis-Joliet house (1683), named after the explorer, gives access to the funicular which whisks you to the Upper Town in a few seconds. But if you feel you need a bit of exercise, walk up, by way of the Côte de la Montagne and Casse-Cou (Breakneck) Steps.

Close to the river bank, there's an interesting Museum of Civilization at 85 Rue Dalhousie, with interactive exhibits. From the old restored port, the Lévis ferry crossing (traverse) is a must, providing an uninterrupted panorama of the city from the deck.

Château Frontenac

At first glance you might easily imagine that the castle dates back to the early days of colonization, when Frontenac himself governed New France with an iron hand. But when you look more closely at the fanciful turrets and verdigris roofs, it's the fairy-tale castles of Louis II of Bavaria that spring to mind. They do, indeed, have something in common, for all of them were built at the end of the 19th century. However, the foundation stone of Château Frontenac was laid not by a mad king, but by a railway company. The grandiose hotel is still a jewel in the crown of the Canadian Pacific Railway, which had it built to accommodate passengers on the first transcontinental train journeys. Take a guided tour to admire the splendid wood panelling, the grand ballroom, and the cafés.

Quebecois and tourists alike stroll up and down Terrasse Dufferin, an elegant wooden walkway alongside the château, taking a pause now and then to drink in the fabulous view over the river. In winter, the wooden boards make a perfect sledge run. The platform goes round the Citadel, becoming the Promenade des Gouverneurs with a number of stairways (closed in winter) leading to the Plains of Abraham (Battlefields Park).

Place d'Armes

At the other end of the terrace is a statue of Champlain. In the shadow of the château, Place d'Armes, a small esplanade with trees and neo-Gothic fountain, opens into the heart of the Upper Town. Here is the Fort Museum, presenting sound-and-light shows illustrating Anglo-French battles, and a 36-sq-m (390-sq-ft) scale model of the town as it was in 1750. In pedestrians-only Rue Sainte-Anne, there are several inviting little restaurants, and a Wax Museum in a house dating from 1640. Perpendicular Rue du Trésor becomes a veritable open-air art gallery in summer. Below the château, Rue Saint-Louis has many restaurants and a number of handsome 18th-century houses. Horse-drawn carriages line up in the square to offer rides around the town.

The Upper Town

Its cobbled lanes are a delight. Among the most pleasant are Rues Couillard, Sainte-Famille and Saint-Flavien. It doesn't matter whether you wander around haphazardly or follow a map; in either case you will come across most of the main attractions. In Rue Buade, Notre-Dame Cathedral stands on the site of the first chapel built by Champlain in 1633. The Seminary, founded 30 years later, is interesting for its interior chapel, which contains the tomb of the first bishop of the city. There's also a Museum of French America covering 400 years with various themed displays: European and Quebecois art, jewellery, and so on. Close at hand, the Town Hall, inaugurated in 1896, marries diverse architectural styles. The Holy Trinity Anglican Cathedral of 1793 is a copy of London's church of Saint-Martin-in-the-Fields.

There are many other museums covering the history, more particularly the religious history, of the city. The Ursuline Museum in Rue Donnacona is housed in a convent founded in 1639; it documents the community's past and its activity among the Iroquois and Algonquin peoples. There is a richly decorated 18th-century chapel. The Augustine convent in Rue Charlevoix was established five years later by three nuns from Dieppe. The nearby Hôtel-Dieu is the oldest hospital on the American continent. Its very fine museum illustrates the life of French Canadians through everyday objects such as furniture, tapestries and, in this particular museum, surgical instruments. At the end of Rue Saint-Jean, the gate of the same name is next to Artillery Park, famous for its relief map of Quebec in 1808. A large garden leads to the ramparts.

The Grande Allée

Through the Saint-Louis gate, rebuilt in 1878 in medieval style, the Parliament building—dating from the same era—houses the Assembly and a gallery of presidential portraits, which you can see on a guided visit.

The Grande Allée Est, originally the path taken by the Hurons coming to Quebec to sell skins, is now an elegant avenue of Victorian houses lined with pavement cafés and restaurants. If you continue westwards, you eventually reach the landscaped gardens of opulent villas stretching as far as Battlefields Park.

The Citadel

Built during the 1840s on ancient French fortifications, the citadel was meant to prevent attack by troops of the United States in case of renewed Anglo-American hostilities. Since 1920 it has been the headquarters of the 22nd regiment and its Royal Museum, which contains arms, uniforms, and so on. Every day at 10 a.m. (unless it is raining!) the Changing of the Guard perpetuates a very British custom, busbies included. In Rue Saint-Denis behind the Château Frontenac, the architecture is typical of Brittany's Saint-Malo. There is a breathtaking view of Quebec and the Saint Lawrence from the promenade.

Battlefields Park

It was here on the Plains of Abraham that French Canada ceased to exist. British troops wiped out those of the Marquis de Montcalm in 1759 and took the town of Quebec. Ironically, both the French and the British generals lost their lives on the battlefield. A statue commemorates the resistance put up by Montcalm. However, time has wrought its changes and the park, overlooking the Saint Lawrence, is a now peaceful place where the Quebecois come to relax. The Quebec Museum, housed in a disused prison, holds an important collection of local art.

The West End

The residential suburb of Sillery has retained several historic buildings. These are the house of the Jesuits in Chemin du Foulon, founded in 1637 to convert and sedentarize the Montagnais and Algonquins and now a museum; the Bagatelle villa, 1563 Chemin Saint-Louis, a magnificent 19th-century dwelling with beautiful gardens and now an exhibition centre; and the Cataraqui estate at no. 2141, completely restored and furnished as in 1850. Laval University is also in Sillery; it's the oldest French university in North America.

At Sainte-Foy, the Aquarium is devoted in particular to fresh- and

Quebec's gourmets are well-acquainted with Rue Saint-Louis, below the château.

saltwater fish of the region. The IMAX dome in Boulevard des Galeries is one of the largest 3-D cinemas in the world.

The King's Road

Before you leave Quebec, stop at the historic Cartier-Brébeuf Park on the north bank of the Saint-Charles River. It commemorates the 1535–36 overwintering of Jacques Cartier and contains a lifesize reproduction of his ship *La Grande Hermine*.

Descending the left bank of the Saint Lawrence, you follow the ancient *chemin du Roy,* the King's Road, along which stand a few venerable dwellings.

Before it flows into the Saint Lawrence, the Montmorency River pours over an impressive cataract 84 m (276 ft) high. The spectacle is at its best at the end of spring and the beginning of summer when the snows have melted, or in winter when it is partially frozen. A small cable-car takes visitors to the country house at the head of the falls, where there are shops and a restaurant.

Ile d'Orléans

So French in name and in appearance, so Quebecois in its soul and history, the Ile d'Orléans is a haven in the middle of the Saint 39

Lawrence. Not long ago, you could only have reached it by boat—or on foot when it was frozen. A bridge has put paid to the island's isolation, which no one regrets except, perhaps, the inhabitants: some of the old-timers, it's whispered, used to dabble in witchcraft… The Quebecois now whip over the river then drive lazily along the country roads, through fields and orchards, savouring the land of their ancestors. In spring whole families come over for "sugaring off" parties.

Inhabited from the very first days of colonization, the island that Jacques Cartier called the Ile de Bacchus has more than 600 listed buildings and is a true architectural treasurehouse. By following the Royal Road laid out around the island in 1744, you discover its different parishes. Sainte-Pétronille, at the west end, was a resort much appreciated by artists in the last century. Rich landowners have left magnificent residences hidden behind red oaks and maples. On the east coast, Saint-Laurent, where British troops disembarked in 1759, was an important riverboat-building centre in the 19th-century. At Saint-Jean, a pretty village with a cluster of coloured roofs, the Mauvide-Genest manor of 1734 is reminiscent of the stone buildings of Normandy. It has an excellent Museum of History and Ethnography. Saint-François, at the most easterly point, lies on the migratory path of the goose. You can view them—or the surrounding landscape if it's the wrong time of year—from an observation tower. Past the tip of the island, the waters of the Saint Lawrence give free rein to their colossal power, held back until now.

On the west coast, the strawberry capital of Sainte-Famille has an astonishing tri-steepled church (1748). But it's Saint-Pierre, just before the bridge back across the Saint Lawrence, that has the oldest (1717) and most beautiful of the island's churches, remodelled in the 19th century.

Huron Country

When Champlain founded Quebec, the first Amerindians he encountered were those canny traders the Hurons. Victims of violent attacks by the Iroquois, they allied themselves to the French. Definitively defeated in 1640, they dispersed throughout the region. For the most part assimilated, scarcely more than a thousand Hurons now live at Wendake, only 15 km (10 miles) from Quebec, their last domain and one of 39 Amerindian reserves in the province.

The communal long houses sheltering several families disappeared long ago, and the last Hurons, nowadays of very mixed parentage, have had to resort to tourism as their main source of income. Nevertheless, the Huron nation has its own flag (a beaver, snowshoes and a canoe), its school, chiefs and police. And, as a reminder of the old days, a reproduction traditional village. Guides explain Huron customs as you pass through the trapper's cabin, the long house, the smokehouse and the "sauna".

The tour is very instructive, and can be rounded off by a visit to the Huron restaurant and the Arouanne Museum. The craftwork on sale in the souvenir shops is generally produced locally.

The Laurentians

The suburbs rapidly give way to a land of forest, mountains and countless lakes: the Quebec Laurentians. The Laurentides Provincial Park, considerably farther north, covers almost 10,000 sq km (4,000 sq miles), one of the largest in the province. Deep in the forest and away from prying eyes, enthusiastic hikers can hope to see black bears, coyotes, lynx and elk, although in general the wildlife is rather shy.

La Beauce

The wooded plains and hills of the Beauce straddle the Chaudière River. One of the latest regions to be colonized because of its distance from the Saint Lawrence, it is nevertheless one of the most fiercely French areas in Quebec. The Beaucerons tap more than half of Quebec's maple sugar and syrup from the rich land (40 per cent of world production). There are few tourist attractions to speak of, other than the Marius-Barbeau Museum of Ethnology in Saint-Joseph-de-Beauce and the large covered footbridge at Notre-Dame-des-Pins.

3 THE MOST BEAUTIFUL ISLANDS Hundreds of islands break the smooth surface of the mighty Saint Lawrence. **Ile d'Orléans** encompasses the very identity of Quebec. **Ile aux Coudres**, perhaps with more right than the others to the name of island, as it is not linked to the mainland by bridge, dreams in the sun. **Ile Verte**, with 40 indomitable inhabitants, floats somewhere between past and present.

THE LOWER SAINT LAWRENCE

Montmagny, Kamouraska, Rivière du Loup,
Ile Verte, Ile aux Basques, Parc du Bic, Rimouski

The configuration of this region, less dramatic than on the opposite bank, draws the eye towards the river. The waters were believed to be good for rheumatism, and Quebec's high society started coming here from the early 19th century; to accommodate them several of the hamlets practically turned into spas. Their reputation endures, but visitors also come for the natural beauties of the river shores, where the sand banks and islets are rich in bird life.

Montmagny

There are a few old dwellings in the town, such as the Couillard-Duplessis house built in 1768 (now the tourist office), or the Gilles Casault house (1750), which looks as though it has been sent over directly from the green fields of Normandy. However, the big attraction in Montmagny is the snow geese: during the migratory season, the banks of the Saint Lawrence and the islands are literally submerged by flocks of thousands of squawking birds. In the middle of October, the ten-day Snow Goose Festival draws all the gourmets, hunters and onlookers of the Lower Saint Lawrence.

The Islands

Offshore, some thirty small islands lay sprinkled like confetti over the vast mirror of the Saint Lawrence: Ile à l'Oignon, Ile du Calumet, Ile de la Sottise, Ile Madame… A ferry serves the Ile aux Grues, the only one inhabited all year round. The 250 inhabitants live mainly from fishing and cheese-making. In winter, when the frozen waters prevent the ferries from leaving the quay, the famous ice canoes take over. You can visit the church, as well as the inn which has found its quarters in the old hunting lodge of Sieur de Montmagny (1650). Walk or cycle to the neighbouring Ile aux Oies (Goose Island), linked by a sandbar except during the spring and autumn equinoctial tides. It is a stopover for thousands of geese migrating south.

The strip of Grosse Ile to the west recalls unhappy memories and shattered hopes. Known as Quarantine Island under British rule, it handled more than 4.5 million prospective immigrants from 1832 to 1937. In 1847, 7,000 Irish immigrants died of

Parc du Bic, a landscape created by an angel.

typhus and were buried here. Along with a few other ruins, their graves are still visible, surmounted by the Celtic cross.

The Region

A few miles from Montmagny, the hamlet of Islet sur Mer gained fame because of the predilection of its men to become sailors. The Bernier Museum pays homage to them. The reputation of Saint-Jean-Port-Joli goes back to the 1930s, when a family of fishermen decided to revive traditional woodcarving. Since then, many others have set up workshops here in the attractive wooden village houses. The Musée des Anciens Canadiens contains figures sculpted by the three Bourgault brothers, representing local personalities. The Médard-Bourgault Museum displays other sculptures, woodwork and furniture. A little further on, La Pocatière has the fine François Pilote ethnological museum illustrating rural life at the beginning of the 20th century.

Kamouraska

In the autumn mists or the spring sunshine, the fishermen's eel-traps placed on the flat bed of the river recall the New France of bygone days. The Aboiteau interpretive centre and the museum demonstrate the ancient skills of the farmers, turned fishermen by force of circumstances. Kamouraska is also known for the original design of its roofs. At low tide, you can walk out to the Kamouraska archipelago. In the early 18th century, they used to stretch nets between the islands to catch white whales.

Rivière du Loup

Forming an amphitheatre on a promontory, Rivière du Loup has lovely views over the Saint Lawrence, at this point more than 20 km (12 miles) wide. Along the shores of the "sea" as it is called here, hotels and second homes bear witness to the attraction this tranquil coast holds for the Quebecois.

To the south, Notre-Dame-du-Portage is reputed for thalassotherapy treatment. Cacouna, to the north, became one of the most fashionable resorts of high society after 1840. Excursions are available to Ile aux Lièvres or Ile du Pot à l'Eau-de-Vie for bird- and whalewatching. A lookout in town provides a view of the Loup River, falling 125 ft (38 m) over a cliff terrace.

Ile Verte

Among the many islands to be named by Jacques Cartier, this was one of the first to be equipped with a lighthouse to guide river traffic. Built in 1809, it is open for visits.

The prosperous-looking houses indicate that the island must have seen better days: the population reached more than 400 in the 1920s. Only forty-odd people still live here, but they vigorously defend their decision to stay and raise lambs on the salt meadows and smoke herring, as in the good old days. In the summer, tourists and locals come to enjoy the peace and to watch the birds in the sanctuary.

Ile aux Basques

The Ile aux Basques was a favourite refuge of Basque whalers in the 17th century. They came to flense the whale carcasses and to melt down the fat to be stored in barrels. On the shore, archaeologists have unearthed the remains of four large stone ovens used for this purpose.

Parc du Bic

When he had created the world, the Great Spirit ordered one of his messengers to decorate it. With one artistic flick of the fingernail, the angel scratched out the bed of the Saint Lawrence then scattered stones and mountains around to make a harmonious landscape. Afterwards, he was left with a heap of boulders, far too cumbersome to carry back to heaven. So he threw them into the river, and thus were born the isles of Bic. Ever since, the green-clad rocks,

populated only by seabirds, have formed a wild and beautiful landscape.

At Cap à l'Orignal and Anse Pilote, a few grey seals make an appearance in the heat of the day to bask in the sunshine. Several hiking trails permit a varied exploration of the three different sectors of the reserve.

Rimouski

As it nears Rimouski, the Saint Lawrence, which reaches a width of some 30 km (19 miles) at this point, seems to forget that it is supposed to be a river. As you walk along the promenade, it gets more and more difficult to see the other side.

In the town, you can visit several art galleries and the half-timbered Lamontagne House, one of the few surviving buildings of its kind in North America.

The village of Pointe-au-Père, 10 km (6 miles) to the east, has a Maritime Museum displaying objects retrieved from one of the worst shipwrecks in seafaring history, not as well known as the sinking of the *Titanic*, two years previously, but just as disastrous. On May 29, 1914, the ferry *Empress of Ireland* was rammed in the middle of the night by a Norwegian cargo ship. Within a few minutes, the ferry went down, taking with it more than a thousand passengers and crew. 45

THE GASPÉ PENINSULA

The river is well and truly forgotten here, where the waves have an Atlantic accent, the shingle, the isolated beaches and the rocks, polished by wind and water, whisper of a seafarers' world. Some even refer to it as another Land's End. Fisheries litter the coast, providing a rare industry in this impoverished land, drawing the population away from the interior and leaving it empty. The Gaspé Peninsula, once the home of the Micmac Indians, has nothing left but its mountains and forests, its solitude—and the clouds scudding across the sky.

The North Coast

Between the cliffs and the Gulf of the Saint Lawrence, the villages of the northern coast huddle at the bottom of lonely valleys. The road follows an itinerary that's sprinkled with names speaking of adventure: Rivière au Renard (Fox River), Ruisseau à Rebours (Back to Front Stream), Manche d'Epée (Sword Handle)…

At Grand-Métis, more than 1,000 varieties of plants grow in the beautiful gardens of the Reford villa, on land originally owned by the president of the Canada Pacific Railway Co. At Matane there is a historical museum and a fascinating fish ladder, where you can watch the salmon travelling upstream in the middle of October. There's an observation tower with portholes so you can see their struggles up close.

From Sainte-Anne-des-Monts, a road leads to the Gaspésie Park, home of the timid woodland caribou. Guided excursions with a naturalist offer the chance to approach them. An outing to the Lac aux Américains reveals stunning countryside. Towards Cloridorme, the *vigneaux*, racks for drying cod, are spread out on the banks exposed to sun and wind. However, overfishing of the Gulf waters has reduced the fish catch by a half.

Forillon National Park

The cliffs of this park, rising from beaches of shingle and grey sand, are the last ramparts of the Gaspé Peninsula. This is where the Appalachians, stretching from Alabama, 2,000 km (1,250 miles) away, finally die and sink beneath the waves.

Near Cap des Rosiers, site of the highest lighthouse in Canada (open for visits), the seabirds nest in high-rise homes with a view of

The life of the cod-fishers of old is demonstrated at Grande Grave.

the sea. In summer, cruises will take you to explore the northern shore and observe the wildlife. From the Bay of Gaspé side, other excursions leave Grande-Grave to approach the schools of whales which come to banquet in the plankton-rich waters. From observation posts along the coast you can scan the horizon through a telescope and try to spot their spouts. In the interior, it is relatively easy to come across beavers.

The reconstructed fishing hamlet of Grande-Grave tells the story of the men and women who caught and dried the cod here at the beginning of the century.

Bay of Gaspé

The history of French Canada started here. In this outstandingly beautiful bay, Jacques Cartier, sheltering his fleet from the storm, disembarked on July 24, 1534. The handsome Museum of the Gaspesian Peninsula at the entrance to the town is dedicated to the history, art and ethnology of the region. Beyond the town, the sea penetrates inland to form numerous small lakes. The view from the road is magnificent.

Percé

This village is famous for its huge, solitary Percé Rock, 86 m (282 ft) high. The principal nat-

47

ural curiosity of the Gaspé Peninsula, Percé (meaning "pierced") once had several arches; all save one have collapsed. At low tide, it is possible to approach this monumental pile of stone, but don't plan on climbing it: that is strictly for the birds. Hills surround the village and the panorama is splendid.

Offshore, the small island of Bonaventure is the site of an enormous gannet colony. At the top of a cliff reached after crossing the island, and some 90 m (295 ft) above the waters of the gulf, 55,000 gannets nest and nurture their chicks from April until October. The birds remain quite unruffled while people observe them from platforms built only a few yards from the nearest nests. Several other species occupy the rest of the island: tridactyl seagulls, black guillemots, Arctic puffins, etc. You can also walk past the abandoned houses and the small graveyard, the resting place of the first colonists who came from Jersey. Boats ply to-and-fro from Percé.

South of Percé, Anse à Beaufils attracts geologists as its shoreline is strewn with pebbles of agate quartz.

Baie des Chaleurs

Jacques Cartier landed in the bay in the summer of 1534. The land is flatter and less rugged than on the north coast, dotted with little villages edged by beaches of shingle or red sand.

At Bonaventure, the Acadian Museum presents the heritage of the Acadians who came here after the expulsion. Not far away, the Maria Reserve is home to a few Micmac families. At New Richmond, the British Heritage Centre is a reconstruction of a Loyalist village of the 18th century.

From the top of Mont-Saint-Joseph, the Baie des Chaleurs can be admired in all its splendour. Near the seaside resort of Carleton sur Mer, at Miguasha Park, a museum has been set up on a fossil site more than 350 million years old.

Matapédia

The funnel-shaped Baie des Chaleurs narrows at Matapédia, closing off the river valley of the same name. The views are wonderful, in particular from the New Brunswick shore. Near Restigouche is a second group of Micmacs, numbering almost 1,000. The community produces high quality craftwork, and there's an art centre. Matapédia Valley is a centre for forest exploitation: temporary loggers' camps, sawmills and paper factories stretch all the way to Sainte-Flavie on the Saint Lawrence. During the Indian summer, the colours here are exceptional.

THE NORTH BANK

Sainte-Anne de Beaupré, Cap Tourmente,
Charlevoix, Tadoussac, The North Coast

Between Quebec and the end of the road lies more than 1,000 km (600 miles) of increasingly wild and lonely countryside. All along the inescapable Saint Lawrence, mountains climb and fall, rent by bays, fields and seemingly infinite forests. A little further, and the boat penetrates into areas which remained uninhabited until very recently. The isolation is extreme and here, even more than elsewhere, the kindliness and hospitality of the Quebecois is proverbial.

Sainte-Anne de Beaupré

The great cathedral of Saint Anne was built only in the 1920s, but the faithful have been flocking here for more than three centuries to climb the stairs of the Scala Santa on their knees. The Paré workshop, 2 km (a mile) away, is a sort of museum of legends, depicted by woodcarvings. The large park of Mont-Sainte-Anne at Beaupré offers all kinds of activities in summer and winter alike. A cable-car leads to the summit from where you can look down on both banks of the Saint Lawrence. At Saint-Joachim, on the way to Charlevoix, the Sainte-Anne Falls tumble into a spectacular "grand canyon".

Cap Tourmente

For most of the time, there's nothing special about Cap Tourmente. But twice a year, a white tornado hits the park. In early October, great squadrons of snow geese from the north land on the shores, covering the sand banks with a tidal wave of feathers. From the observation post at Bois-sent-bon, you can see nothing but heaving flocks of birds: up to 100,000 have been counted at times. A shot resounds or a plane flies over, and there's general panic as they all lift off at once into the sky, so many that their wings sometimes collide. Groups spread out, flying low over the river, skimming the reddening foliage of the trees set aglow by the Indian summer.

The snow geese come back in spring but scatter more along the river banks and make a less spectacular display. Try to see them in October, if you can, especially if you want to take photos.

Charlevoix

A giant meteorite estimated at 15,000 million tons crashed into the north bank of the Saint Lawrence some 300 million years ago. The shock produced a crater 60 km (38 miles) in diameter,

The basilica of Sainte-Anne-de-Beaupré, a hallowed place of pilgrimage.

forming what is now known as Mont des Eboulements ("landslide mountain") at the centre, resulting from the rebound of the earth's crust after the impact. This region of Canada has always been the most prone to earth tremors. The scenic coastal strip of farmland known as Charlevoix, on the brink of the great northern wilderness, was classed by UNESCO in 1988 as a World Biosphere Reserve. Forest, taiga, tundra and peat make it one of the nation's most ecologically diverse regions. With a small population and poor communications, Charlevoix was for a long time largely ignored by New France.

A happy consequence is that traditions were maintained and it is now a favourite region of Quebec. Known for its good life, its hospitality, and its attractive white houses, it continues to inspire artists from all parts of the province.

Baie Saint-Paul

Developed after 1680 under the protection of the monks of the Quebec Seminary, this parish has remained one of the most traditional in the Province. Nestling in its valley, the town is the haunt of many of Quebec's artists, as bear witness its numerous galleries and dynamic cultural scene. The work of local painters is displayed in the arts and exhibition centres. The natural history centre is open only in summer.

Saint-Joseph de la Rive

Opposite the Ile aux Coudres, this pretty village is squeezed between the mountain and the Saint Lawrence. Old-time schooners which sailed the river and set the rhythm of life until the dawn of the 20th century are being restored here. Thanks to their shallow draught, they could be drawn onto the beach at high tide and unloaded by horse-and-cart at low tide. The old shipyard has been converted into a museum. Perpetuating another tradition, the Saint-Gilles paper mill produces paper from cotton pulp using 17th-century methods, embedded with dried leaves and flowers. A small museum presents the manufacture and uses of paper.

Ile aux Coudres

Schooners washed up on the beach, stone houses and windmills… the Ile aux Coudres has retained something of the atmosphere of early New France. Named by Jacques Cartier for its hazelnut trees (*"couldres"* in old French), the island was for many years inhabited only by seminarists. Then it became a major schooner-building centre. From

their custom of wearing boots of white whaleskin, the islanders became known as *marsouins* (porpoises).

The island is a very popular destination for the inhabitants of Quebec city who come here to get away from it all at weekends. At Saint-Louis, two mills built in 1824 and 1836, one driven by water and the other by wind, used

---

MIGRATING GEESE

The snow geese breed in the Far North, where they arrive at the beginning of May. They have only three months of short Arctic summer to lay, hatch and fatten their young. In the last days of August, they all leave to fly south, heading for the east coast of America. The journey of 4,000 km (2,500 miles), even with speeds reaching up to 95 kph (60 mph), requires at least one stopover, sometimes several. At the beginning of October, 450,000 snow geese land on the Saint Lawrence shores. The tidal currents and the combination of fresh and salt water produce abundant food. The geese rest for a while, feed, then set off once more. The cycle is completed when they return the following spring, on their way back to their northerly breeding grounds.

to take it in turns to make flour. In spring, the watermill driven by the melt-water of the snows was the most efficient; in winter freezing conditions made windpower the only possibility. Restored and now in working order, they grind flour which is on sale in the museum shop.

Not far away, the museum of water transport (Musée Les voitures d'eau) revives the romance of navigation on the Saint Lawrence. In the village of La Baleine, the museum in the Leclerc house of 1750 presents artefacts and furniture of the island.

Parc des Grands-Jardins

Inland, this section of the Charlevoix biosphere is carpeted with the coniferous forest of the taiga. A fragment of the Far North on the doorstep of Quebec, it may give you the chance to catch a glimpse of caribou—there's a small herd here, which is unusual at this latitude. On the whole, however, the animals are timid and keep to themselves.

Eastern Charlevoix

The attractive village of Les Eboulements perched above the Saint Lawrence has a mill two

Geese take time out on the tidal reaches of the Saint Lawrence before continuing their journey.

centuries old. At Pointe-au-Pic, next to an 18-hole golf course, the Manoir Richelieu, a luxurious hotel and casino dating from the beginning of the 20th century, was built for passengers from the river's busy steamboat trade. The recent Charlevoix Museum presents the area's history and its artists.

La Malbaie ("Bad Bay"), at the mouth of the river of the same name, was so called by Champlain who ran aground here. Across the bay, Cap-à-l'Aigle has a pleasant architectural harmony. Port-au-Persil ("Parsley Port"), futher north, is charmingly set on a bay overlooked by a spur of forest. Baie Sainte-Catherine, just before you reach the mouth of the saltwater Saguenay River, is a lumber village and centre for whalewatching cruises and excursions upstream.

Tadoussac

There was a time when Tadoussac was considered as the Eldorado of all the French ports on the Atlantic. During the first half of the 17th century, the warehouse handled 15,000 to 20,000 beaver skins during any one season. This highly lucrative trade attracted adventurers of all kinds. They still tell the tale of a boatload of passengers newly arrived from Europe, weary of the long voyage and in such a hurry to set foot on 53 shore that they disembarked onto the backs of a school of whales, so numerous that they blocked the river. Boat trips are available for whalewatching and explorations of the Saguenay, cleft so deeply into the rock that its steep sides give it the appearance of a fjord.

The Centre

Tadoussac is a sizeable, attractive village with many houses built of wood. You can visit the charming chapel set up for the Indians in 1747, as well as the reconstructed log cabin of Pierre Chauvin from Dieppe, founder of the first trading post in the time of France's Henri IV. It houses displays on the Montagnais Indians.

Before leaving for your cruise, a detour by way of the Marine Mammal Centre will help you learn to distinguish between beluga, finback, blue whale, humpback and rorqual.

Whalewatching

In the Gulf of Saint Lawrence, the waters of the ocean, driven by the cold Labrador Current, flow up along the coast through the underwater Laurentian Channel some 300 m (1000 ft) deep. At Tadoussac, the sea water strikes a rocky sill that forces it up to the surface, stirring the depths and bringing to higher levels the micro-organisms on which plankton and krill feed and multiply, creating a well-stocked larder for the whales.

In April, the whales leave the warm seas of their breeding grounds and return northwards. From May until October, hundreds take advantage of the rich waters of the river to build up their fat reserves: the rare blue whale, 28–30 m (90–100 ft) long, which consumes 4 tons of krill per day; the rorqual and rarer sperm whale, both reaching 20 m (65 ft); the non-migratory beluga or white whale… ten species in all. It is an uncommon privilege to be able to approach these creatures so closely. From May until October, daily excursions by rubber dinghy, large boat or even turn-of-the-century schooner, offer three hours exploration of the confluence of the Saint Lawrence and the Saguenay. With luck, you may even spot humpback whales leaping out of the waves. Dress warmly, even in summer.

The North Coast

Abutting the wide open spaces of Quebec's North, the regions of Manicouagan, Mingan and Duplessis were long closed to colonization. The whole area was part of the Domaine des Postes du Roi, reserved for trappers in the employ of the state, and the first settlers did not come until 1850. There are towns along the coast,

The windmill on the Ile aux Coudres is still in operation.

but the interior is essentially devoid of human life. Only Quebec's grand hydroelectric projects have opened up a few tracts of the territory.

Manicouagan

As you follow the Saint Lawrence downstream, one magnificent view follows another. Near the cliffs of Grandes Bergeronnes, whales swim close enough to be seen with the naked eye. The Betsiamites Reserve, created in 1860, became the "capital" of the Montagnais Indians; they hold a festival every year on August 15. Comeau Bay is the port of access to the Manic-Out-ardes hydroelectric complex. The dam called Manic 5, 215 km (134 miles) inland, is a giant work of art in keeping with the grandeur of the landscape. After Pointe-des-Monts, the Saint Lawrence is a river no longer.

Duplessis

Sept-Iles, named after the six, not seven, islands out in its bay, is a busy port where they transfer grain from lakers to ocean-going vessels. Iron and titanium ore extracted in Labrador 600 km (375 miles) to the north is transported here by an endless chain of goods trains, along one of the world's most northerly railways. 55

From the valley of the River Moisie to the 70-m (230-ft) Tonkas Falls, the train crosses landscapes of incomparable beauty and grandeur. At Schefferville, the first of the mining towns in the wilderness, the terminus looks lost and forlorn. However, this is not Quebec, but Labrador.

At Sept-Iles itself, the only trace of the past is the log fort built by Sieur Joliet in 1662 and reconstructed here with all its outbuildings. Ile de Grande Basque, offshore, criss-crossed with educational hiking trails, is open to visitors. Here you will see the birds, the peat bogs and carnivorous plants that the American painter Audubon discovered in 1833.

At the beginning of August, you can attend the Innu Nikamu festival of Amerindian dance and music, held in the Maliotenam Reserve.

Mingan

The road finally comes to an end at Havre Saint-Pierre, 1,100 km (690 miles) from Montreal. Offshore, the forty-odd limestone islands and islets of the Mingan Archipelago form a magnificent national park which is a sanctuary for a rich flora and numerous seabirds, among them colourful puffins. Amazing rock formations sculpted by wind, water and ice punctuate the coast. Known to the locals as "flowerpots", some of these eroded monoliths have been given inspired names like "the wolf and the lamb", the "Indian gate", and so on. With its peat bogs, its dwarf forest, the drift-

---

SOS BELUGAS

Estimated at 5,000 at the beginning of the century, the white whales (belugas) of the Saint Lawrence are now reduced to fewer than 500. This whale, 5 m (16 ft) long, lives only here and in the icy waters of the Far North. It is the only cetacean species which is sedentary. Hunting is illegal, the beluga has no predators—only the poor state of the river can be blamed for its decline. Postmortem examination of whale cadavers has revealed the presence of 24 chemical pollutants. One-third of the new-born whales seem to suffer malformations. In 1992, an international campaign, "Adopt a white whale", was launched in order to gather funds for research. Any group or individual wishing to help save a beluga could adopt one at a price of $5,000 each. The price includes the right to name your own animal. Octavius, Snow-White and Vagabond are already spoken for…

wood washed up onto its shingle beaches, and its seals, Quarry is without doubt the most beautiful of the islands. In summer, the research station offers beginners' courses in the study of whales—many of which cruise offshore—permitting you to become truly familiar in theory and in practice with these gentle giants.

The Lower North Coast

Although the road is scheduled to reach Natashquan, for the time being the lower north coast is still largely preserved from contact with the outside world. The only access is by air or by sea—and in winter by snowmobile. All summer, the *Nordic Express* ferry plies from port to port, livening up the isolated communities of fishermen who are all still pioneers at heart.

At Natashquan, "the place where bears are hunted" in the Montagnais language, the Indian Reserve of coloured houses lies next to the village, surrounded by islets of pink granite. The church, decorated by Amerindians, is delightful: its walls are adorned with snowshoes, dog sleds, fish and harpoons.

Beyond Natashquan, hamlets become fewer and fewer and dwindle in size. After Kegaska comes Ouapitagone and then Harrington Harbour, this last inhabited all year round by English-speaking seafarers. It clings to the naked and polished rock of a barren islet. To make the going easier, wooden walkways lead from house to house.

The ferry reaches the end of its voyage at Blanc Sablon. Once there, you can retrace your route or cross the Strait of Belle Isle. Just opposite lies Newfoundland, less than two hours away by boat. But that's another story…

4 THE FOUR MOST BEAUTIFUL RESERVES Whereas Europe's fauna has greatly diminished in numbers, the New World remains rich in wildlife. Along the coast, gannets on **Ile Bonaventure** and puffins on the **Mingan Archipelago** nest in their thousands only a few feet from human visitors. At **Cap Tourmente**, the snow geese put on a show which seems little short of a mirage. In the heart of the forest, the animals are harder to see. Spotting a rare woodland caribou in the **Gaspésie Park** is just reward for those who have the patience to wait.

THE ISLANDS
Anticosti Island, Magdalen Islands

Anticosti, 135 km (85 miles) from the north coast, is more or less the size of Corsica. Its rugged coastline has long been feared by sailors, and not without reason: more than 400 boats have gone to a watery grave in this "graveyard of the gulf". Nowadays a hunting and fishing reserve, the island is an immense tract of spruce forest laced by rushing waterways.

Eroded by the surf, the Magdalen Archipelago is falling to pieces. The waves pound the red, ochrous sandstone cliffs with such strength that these are crumbling to sand, swept by the wind into enormous, romantic dunes. The elements have shaped them according to their whim, lining them up to stitch together six of the seven inhabited islands and hemming them all with 300 km (190 miles) of deserted beach.

At the beginning of spring, the thaw brings icebergs from Greenland. This is the time to go out on the ice. Colonies of seals float on the cracking ice floes, hunted in small numbers for generations.

Anticosti Island
Conceded by Louis XIV to Louis Joliet in 1680, Anticosti Island was never very profitable and ultimately changed hands several times. Then, one day in 1895, fate brought an eccentric millionaire to its shores in the shape of the French chocolate manufacturer Henri Menier, a fanatical hunter and a philanthropist whenever the fancy took him. For years he had been travelling the world on his yacht searching for the lost island of his childhood dreams. For the sum of $125,000, Menier bought Anticosti and became "Baron Cocoa".

A bit of a dictator, somewhat paternalistic, he founded the village of Baie Sainte-Claire before removing the inhabitants further along the coast to his "capital", Port-Menier. Local rules of a sort were promulgated, forbidding hunting and drinking. In 1916, Menier introduced a few deer from Virginia into the island, to make sport for himself and a few friends. He also brought the telephone, built a road and installed a railway line for the forestry. He even struck his own coinage. Unfortunately, his death intervened and the island was sold in 1925. It was finally bought by the government of Quebec in 1974.

Port-Menier
Virtually the entire population of 300 lives in the island's only village, Port-Menier on the edge of Gamache Bay. Nothing remains

Anticosti Island attracts hunters and photographers alike.

of its golden age. The railway line has been swallowed by the forest and Menier's "Norman Castle", a magnificent hunting lodge, went up in smoke. The ecomuseum has retained a few items of furniture, along with naturalized animals and a presentation of the island's history.

Around the Island

Although Anticosti's principal attractions are hunting and fishing, you don't have to indulge in these pastimes to enjoy the landscape and observe the wildlife. The 220 white-tailed deer originally imported by Menier have now swelled to more than 100,000. Some 5,000 elks share the forest with them, not to mention otters and 215 species of bird. A 100-km (60-mile) road and a few forest paths enable you to penetrate to the island's heart.

At the western point, the forlorn remains of Baie Sainte-Claire—dilapidated huts and graveyards—are slowly being devastated by the elements: it's a real ghost village. On the north coast, the lighthouse at Carleton Head offers a panorama of the Jacques Cartier Strait, frequented in summer by numbers of whales.

Deep in the hill overlooking Patate River, a cave of the same name has a chamber 10 m (33 ft) 59 high and a "Curtain Room" (Salle des Draperies), reached by a narrow passage 80 m (260 ft) long.

In the interior, Lake Wickenden is celebrated for its fossils, 400 million years old. Continuing eastwards, the track passes the canyon of Observation River, locked in a rocky valley. A little further, and you see the Vauréal River, hurling itself with abandon down a fall of 76 m (250 ft). Reached by boat, the southeast headland, at the foot of impressive cliffs, is the chosen domain of a large colony of seals.

Magdalen Islands

The Amerindian name for these islands is Menagoesenog, "the wave-swept isles". They once hunted walrus here. Colonization of the islands really began only in 1755 with the arrival of Acadian refugees from the expulsion. Towards 1792 more fugitives joined them, French and Scottish settlers from Saint-Pierre and Miquelon where they had been caught up in revolutionary troubles. Each group established its own territory, English-speakers on Ile d'Entrée and Grosse Ile, and the French (who call the islands the Iles de la Madeleine) everywhere else.

Two centuries later, nothing has changed. The 700 descendants of the Scottish settlers are still in the same place, along with 14,000 Magdalenians (Madelinots) of Acadian ancestry. The islanders are first and foremost fishermen—the waters of the Labrador Gulf are among the richest in the world. Furthermore, this is the world's lobster capital. The houses, green like the fields, blue like the sea and red like the shellfish, form optimistic spots of colour in the valleys. This corner of the world embodies the perpetual dilemma—it's a beautiful place to live, but so hard to make a living.

From Isle to Isle

The ferries tie up at Ile du Cap-aux-Meules, home of half the population of the islands. Behind the large wooden church of La Vernière, a historic monument, a footpath leads to the summit of La Butte du Vent. The panorama takes in the entire archipelago: to the north the coastal stretch and Ile Grande-Entrée; to the south the Baie de Plaisance and Ile de Havre-Aubert. Follow Chemin des Caps to enjoy a succession of invigorating seascapes, wind and seaspray guaranteed. At the Gros-Cap headland, a red sandstone arch stands elegantly on the pale sand.

Havre-Aubert, the most southerly isle, is the site of the first French colony in the 16th century, and later of the first colony of refugees from Acadia. The

Musée de la Mer displays mementoes of the old days. These are a record of the 400 shipwrecks which have brought a great deal of sorrow to these island communities. The eastern end of Havre-Aubert, known as Sandy Hook, is the scene of an extraordinary sandcastle competition every summer. A different route leads you to the heel of Havre-Aubert and its scattered houses facing the sea.

If you feel the need to warm up after all that fresh air, then drop in at the Café de la Grave, the meeting place of the entire village. A ferry crosses the Baie de Plaisance to the tiny Ile d'Entrée, where all 200 inhabitants (but one) are English-speaking.

North of Cap-aux-Meules, the Ile du Havre-aux-Maisons is the headquarters of Magdalenian mariners. Although the herring smokehouses have now attained the status of historic monuments, huge mussel beds are still maintained.

On the Ile aux Loups, the Chemin des Montants meanders gently past a string of sand dunes. In the extreme north of the archipelago, the 500 English-speaking inhabitants of Grosse Ile make a living from fishing and from salt. A mine opened in the 1970s exploits a seam of salt situated 200 m (650 ft) under the sea. The hamlet of Old Harry, all painted white, has great charm. The village school has been turned into a museum retracing the history of the Scottish community.

On the north side, a path leads to the beach of Grande-Echouerie stretching 9 km (6 miles) to the eastern headland, a seabird sanctuary. Offshore, Ile Brion and the Rocher aux Oiseaux, difficult to reach, are also protected. Grande-Entrée, the last island, has the principal lobster port of the whole group.

5 **THE MOST BEAUTIFUL VILLAGES** Wooden houses clustered around a white church are typical of Quebec's villages and embody the charm of New France. In the Lower Saint Lawrence region, **Saint-Jean-Port-Joli** and **Kamouraska** follow this style. On the north coast, the delightful **Port-au-Persil** offers a friendly welcome. The same is true at **Harrington Harbour** and **Old Harry**, English-speaking villages of the lower north coast and the Magdalen Islands, respectively, with the added attraction of remoteness and sea breezes.

THE NORTH

The last civilized territory before the confines of the great northern forest, the region of Saguenay–Lac-Saint-Jean already lives at a northern rhythm. In winter, snow-mobiles are more common than cars. In summer, the region is inviting to lovers of the outdoors, who will enjoy the rivers, the immense lake and the warm welcome.

Saguenay–Lac-Saint-Jean

Perhaps this is the legendary kingdom of the Saguenay, a kind of Eldorado much searched for in the 16th century but never discovered.

Travelling up the chief tributary of the Saint Lawrence, you cross the threshold of a nature reserve. Along both river banks, a magnificent landscape of forest and dark waters unfolds. The most extensive panorama is revealed at the turning of a minor road at Sainte-Rose-du-Nord, where there's a small nature museum. But to make the most of this experience, stop at the Rivière-Eternité interpretive centre on the south slope. Footpaths lead to the superb river valley of the same name. The views of the cliffs dropping straight into the icy waters of the Saguenay at Cap de la Trinité and Cap Eternité are unequalled. A little further and you reach Ha! Ha! Bay. Opinions differ as to the origin of the name, but the majority seem to think that it represents the ecstatic sighs of the people who first came across it. The Fjord Museum has ethnological exhibits.

Chicoutimi

Occupying both banks of the Saguenay where the fjord narrows, the "Queen of the North" is a surprisingly large town for this latitude. The Saguenay Museum on Rue Jacques-Cartier has a fine collection of Amerindian objects. You might like to see the house of Arthur Villeneuve, a barber who took up painting after his retirement in the 1950s. At 669 Rue Taché Ouest, his home is painted from tip to toe, inside and out, in a cheerful, naive style. The old Pulperie, a pulp mill founded in 1898, summarizes the beginning of the region's economic history. A film made in 1915 on the manufacture of paper pulp is shown in summer. But the high point is the view of the Saguenay rapids.

The Lake

The ancient, circular, glaciated lake covering 1,000 sq km

Forest and lakes, the Saguenay encapsulates Quebec.

(390 sq miles) lies at the heart of a region where the pioneers were forced to adapt their agriculture to the vicissitudes of the climate. At the end of summer, bilberries (here called *bleuets*) are gathered, and this, together with cheese-making, are the principal local industries. A poor region for many years, it is now revitalized by a growth of the tourist industry. The increase in Quebec's population has brought throngs of citizens to the lake shore in search of life's simple pleasures. In August, the more audacious meet up for the celebrated swim across the lake, 32 km (20 miles) there and back.

From Alma you can take pleasure cruises on the lake. At Pointe Taillon Park, a beach some 6 km (4 miles) long provides an opportunity to bathe and to observe the bird life. The park also offers dunes, peat bogs, forests and marshland of great beauty.

Péribonka is home to the Louis-Hémon Museum dedicated to the author of the novel *Maria Chapdelaine*. At Sainte-Jeanne d'Arc there is a wooden mill dating from 1907. Mistassini, the bilberry capital, also houses the Notre-Dame Monastery, known for its chocolate factory. Dolbeau is the site of a centre for astronomy, while Saint-Félicien has a 63

MARIA CHAPDELAINE

The works of French author Louis Hémon (1880–1913) introduced Canada to generations of French people. His best-selling *Maria Chapdelaine* relates the early days of the territory, the daily routine of a rural society steeped in religion. It's a nostalgic love story, too, revealing the pioneering traditions and willpower of a people ready to make sacrifices.

zoo presenting Canadian fauna. A small train takes you (in a cage) for a ride among the animals, which roam free. There is also a reconstruction of a trading post and a trappers' camp, and so on.

Pointe Bleue

Mashteuiatsh, the best-known of the Montagnais villages, is firmly entrenched in the 20th century. The Amerindians live in small wooden houses and many have forgotten the language of their ancestors. Traces of the past are preserved in the Amerindian Museum, or revealed in the souvenir shop, selling traditional handicrafts. The interpretive centre of the Robertson family's fur-trading post recalls the days of the trappers. If you're feeling adventurous, spend a few days in the forest with a Montagnais guide.

Val-Jalbert

On the south side of the lake, the historic village of Val-Jalbert is in fact a logging camp abandoned in 1928. Numerous log cabins have been restored and some are open to the public, but there's a Disneyesque feel about it all. Nothing has altered the Ouiatchouan Falls, tumbling prettily from 72 m (236 ft) behind the old ruined mill.

Chibougamau

The north brings you directly face-to-face with Quebec's wilderness. Wooded hills stretch as far as the eye can see, and the lakes are countless. Chibougamau is the final frontier, or if you prefer, the gateway to the wide open spaces. By the shores of Lake Mistassini, a few Cree Indians lead a modern life, only a few paddle strokes away from their past. When they've had enough of the world of the paleface, they return to their wigwams on their sacred island, forbidden to outsiders.

New Quebec

With the exception of the extreme south of James Bay, all of New Quebec belongs to the Far North:

Four hundred steps (and a cable-car) lead to the top of the Ouitchouan Falls.

taiga, tundra and permafrost mark the territory as it nears the 62nd parallel, the northern frontier of Quebec. Rivers and lakes account for very nearly half of the land surface.

No one travels by road; there are no roads to travel. As distances are great—very great—the only method of transport is the amphibious aircraft. More local-ly, for the Inuit peoples in the north and the Cree in the south, the dog sled or the snowmobile are used. Everyone chooses his own path; there is plenty of space. Reduced to statistics, New Quebec is a surface area of 902,000 sq km (352 000 sq miles), with 20,000 inhabitants spread among 8 Cree villages and 14 Inuit settlements.

James Bay

Not so long ago, whalers used to call in at Whale Post to flense their catch. Also known as Poste de la Baleine in French, Kuujjuarapik in Inuktituk and Whapmagoostui in Cree, this modern settlement, which serves as capital of the territory of James Bay, is home to 1,000 Amerindians. There are 12,000 Cree living in this part of New Quebec; their traditional lands extended from Saskatchewan in central Canada to the mouth of the Great Whale River northeast of James Bay.

The Inuit (don't call them Eskimo, a pejorative term meaning "eater of raw meat") are here at the southern limit of their lands. The area may look peaceful, but it is undergoing a crisis. Cree and Inuit have banded together to oppose the development projects of Hydro-Quebec, and have managed to stop, at least for the time being, the advance of the work.

CREE BELIEFS

Originally hunters of elk and caribou, for generations the Cree followed the migrating herds. When game was scarce, they left in small groups for new hunting grounds. Winter was the best season as the animal tracks were easier to follow in the snow. If it became necessary to kill a bear, the Cree hunter first asked its pardon. He would light a pipe and blow the smoke in the animal's direction to calm its anger. Like all Amerindian tribes, the Cree hunted only out of necessity. Their belief was that Chuetenshu, the North Wind, punished those who showed cruelty to animals by causing them to die of cold. The Cree still hunt nowadays, in part to feed their families, but probably even more to renew their links with their past.

Hudson Bay

North of James Bay the vegetation is entirely tundra. Trees become increasingly rare, with here and there the green smudges of the last stunted willows dotting a landscape of chaotic rocks polished by erosion. At the end of summer, the shores of Hudson Bay is stained with the purple of lichens. This is the migratory season of the caribou, revered by the Inuit. For them, every part of the caribou has a use: flesh, fat, bone, skin, antler. Opposite the Belcher Islands is one of the rare villages of the eastern shore of the bay, Umiujaq, populated by Inuit who have left Whale Post in search of a lifestyle closer to that of their ancestors.

The Ungava Peninsula

Right in the north you enter the world of the aurora borealis. The Ungava Peninsula tops New Quebec and closes Hudson Bay to the east. If you would like to drive a dog sled, to fish or simply if you have an explorer's soul, then this is the place to satisfy your dreams of the Far North. From the air, you may see the strange natural phenomenon which pockmarks the tundra, the New Quebec crater.

HYDRO-QUEBEC

In the 1970s, the federal government launched what some have termed the "project of the century": a succession of dams across the rivers of northern Quebec, with the aim of fulfilling all Canada's needs in electricity and even of exporting whatever was left over to the United States. The only fly in the ointment was the colossal size of the undertaking: the reservoirs created by the dams would flood thousands of square kilometres of virgin territory—Indian lands.

The first phase of the operation, "James Bay I", on La Grande River, created four huge reservoirs flooding 3,000 sq km (1,200 sq miles) of forest. As the region is as flat as a pancake, there was nothing to stop the water from spreading. For the Cree Indians of Shisasibi at the mouth of the waterway, it's the equivalent of London being submerged by the Thames. To avoid the same fate, the population of Whale Post is trying to halt the second phase of the operation. They are supported by 16,000 Cree and Inuit united in the same struggle. If they fail, they will have lost a part of their resources. The caribou will no longer come: their migratory route crosses the land condemned to disappear.

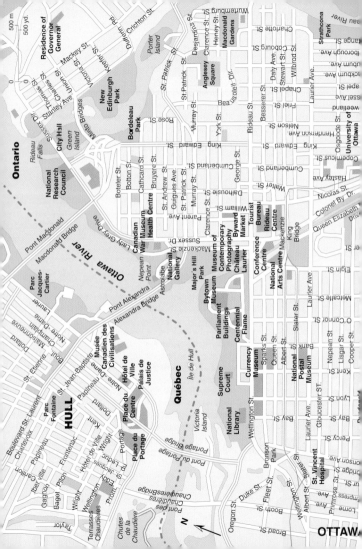

EXCURSIONS
Ottawa, Niagara Falls, Toronto

The federal capital was founded in 1827 during the reign of King George IV, and its growth has kept pace with that of Canada. The centre of political life, Ottawa lies along the Outaouais River which forms the boundary between Quebec to the east and Ontario to the west.

Toronto is the richest city of Canada, benefiting from a dynamic history and its situation on the north shore of Lake Ontario, at the crossroads of Quebec, the United States and the Great Plains. It is the centre of Canadian finance, and its stock market is one of the most important of the North American continent. Like its skyscrapers, Toronto is an overwhelming, dazzling city.

Ottawa

The city is anchored in Ontario, but the presence of Hull, across the river in Quebec, makes the location doubly symbolic and justifies its choice as site of the capital of this bilingual country. The town has remained very British. Gothic buildings, Parliament Hill, the Changing of the Guard, all provide a special atmosphere which comes as a warm and pleasant surprise. Ottawa is not cold and soulless, but beautiful, lively and airy.

Parliament Hill

The three Parliament buildings facing the river were erected between 1859 and 1865 then restored in 1916 after a fire. They form an impressive, harmonious whole. Debate about the architectural style continues: the French maintain it looks English, the English argue that it is of French inspiration. The only certainty is that it is neo-Gothic—perhaps a happy blend of both cultures. You can visit the interior on a guided tour. From the top of the Peace Tower with its renowned peal of bells, the magnificent panorama stretches as far as the Outaouais forest in clear weather. All through the summer, the Changing of the Guard at 10 a.m. attracts crowds of spectators.

Further to the west are the Supreme Court and the National Library.

The City Centre

The triangular Confederation Square is the heart of the city. It contains the National Centre for the Arts, one of the largest cultural groupings in Canada, with theatre, opera and concert halls. The esplanade lies alongside the Rideau Canal, dug in the 1820s to link the Saint Lawrence with the Outaouais River.

In summer, boat trips give you a fish-eye view of the city. In winter, the canal freezes to becomes the longest skating-rink in the world. The Château Laurier Hotel by the river is one of the ostentatious palaces built at the end of the last century by the Canadian railways. Mackenzie Avenue and Sussex Drive, parallel to it, have several big department stores. A stone's throw away are the Byward Market and the basilica of Notre-Dame. Further out, beyond the Rideau River, you come to the first smart residential areas, including Rockcliffe where the Governor General of Canada resides in Rideau Hall.

The Museums

Spacious and luminous, the modern Museum of Fine Art contains an important collection of landscapes by Canadian members of the Group of Seven. There is also a wide range of European paintings from the 16th century up to the present. The German school is particularly well-represented. The unusual chapel of the Convent of the Sœurs Grises de la Croix (Grey Sisters of the Cross) has been moved from Rue Rideau to the first floor of this building.

Ottawa has many other museums: Ski (on Sussex), Photography (by the Rideau Canal), Natural Sciences (McLeod Street south of the city), Science and Technology (Saint-Laurent Bvd), Post Office (Wellington Street), Aviation (Rockcliffe Airport), and more.

Hull

On the Quebec side, Hull embodies the French aspect of the capital. The very handsome Canadian Museum of Civilizations presents the multicultural heritage of the country. Various exhibitions consecrated to the different Amerindian peoples are fascinating.

Niagara Falls

It is difficult to approach Niagara Falls without having qualms. What of the artificial illuminations, the honeymoon hype and the garish trappings of the tourist trade (12 million visitors per year)? You only need to turn your back on it all and simply admire the magnificent spectacle of a huge, white wall of water thundering incessantly over the limestone cliffs, slowly gnawing them away.

Formed by the Niagara River flowing from Lake Erie to Lake Ontario lower down, the Falls form two cascades gushing at a

Capacious yellow waterproofs keep out the worst of Niagara's deluge.

rate of 34 million gallons of water per minute. The American Falls, 300 m (1,076 ft) wide, are separated from the more spectacular Canadian Horseshoe Falls, 800 m (2,600 ft) wide, by Goat Island. You can contemplate them from above, below, or beside. Several towers afford a bird's-eye view, notably the Skylon Tower in Robinson Street, the Minolta Tower on Oakside Drive, or the Maple Leaf Observation Tower in Maple Leaf Village.

In winter, the spray freezes, to magical effect. The classic excursion on board the *Maid of the Mist* brings you as close to the falls as the seething waters will allow. The trip is exciting, deafening—and you'll get drenched (raincoats are provided).

If you cross Rainbow Bridge to the American side, you walk through Queen Victoria Park to Table Rock House, where lifts descend to tunnels cut in the cliff face. You don a yellow raincoat before venturing into the tunnels where openings permit a close-up view of the pounding waters from behind. This is the nearest you can get to the falls, unless you prefer to go over by barrel. Some have actually survived that adventure, as witnessed by the exhibits in the Niagara Falls Museum on River Road. But none of those who tried a kayak lived to tell the tale. To find out how it feels, Ride Niagara enables you to share the thrill from the safety of a simulator.

Toronto

The Huron used to gather here before setting off on the warpath. In their language Toronto means "meeting place". The French built a fort here in 1720, and destroyed it shortly afterwards, leaving the site to the British. First a trading post, then a centre of Puritan colonization, the town grew especially after 1849 when it was declared to be the capital of United Canada (the union of Quebec and Ontario). During the industrial development of the Great Lakes region in the 1870s, Toronto became an economic centre, which it remains to this day.

However, Toronto is not only a window onto the Great Lakes. It is also, perhaps principally, the archetypal cultural melting-pot of the new Canada, or as the Canadians prefer to say, a mosaic society. Forty percent of its 4.5 million inhabitants were born outside Canada: 150,000 Portuguese, 300,000 Chinese and many Russians, Italians, Vietnamese, Indians, and so on. To illustrate the point, CHIN radio station broadcasts in 32 languages. This cosmopolitan Toronto has developed a new and extrovert personality. The sobriety and timidity of the

DOWNTOWN TORONTO

Bloor St. W. · Croft St. · Major St. · Robert St. · Sussex Ave. · Washington Ave. · Huron St. · St. George St. · Spadina Ave. · Bloor St. W.

Royal Ontario Museum

Gardiner Museum of Ceramic Art

YORKVILLE VILLAGE

Metro Toronto Library

Bloor St. E. · Hayden St. · Charles St. · St. Marys St. · Isabella St. · Church St. · Jarvis St.

McLaughlin Planetarium

Roberts Library

Harbord St. · Ulster St. · Classic Ave. · Willcocks St. · Hoskin Ave. · Taddle Creek Rd. · Queen's Park

Queen's Park

St. Joseph St. · Phipps St. · Breadalbane St. · Gloucester St. · Dundonald St. · Wellesley St. · Maitland St. · Alexander St. · Wood St.

University of Toronto

Bancroft Ave. · Russel St. · Spadina Cres. · Kings College Rd. · Queen's Park Cres.

Parliament Buildings

Grosvenor St. · Grenville St. · Carlton St. · Granby St. · McGill St.

College St. · Oxford St. · Nassau St. · Baldwin St. · Wales Ave. · Dundas St. W.

Huron St. · Ross St. · Cecil St. · Beverly St. · Henry St. · McCaul St. · Murray St. · Elm St. · College St. · Hayter St. · Walton St. · Elm St. · Gerrard St.

Ontario Hydro

Orde St. · Gerrard St. · University Ave. · Bay St. · Yonge St. · Keefe Lane · Victoria St. · Gould St. · Church St. · Dalhousie St. · Mutual St. · Jarvis St.

Kensington Market

Alexandra Park · Ryerson Ave. · Denison Ave. · Augusta Ave. · Cameron St. · Spadina Ave.

Art Gallery of Ontario

Grange Park

CHINATOWN

The Grange

Sullivan St. · Phoebe St. · Bulwer St. · D'Arcy St. · Beverly St. · St. Patrick St. · Simcoe St.

Campbell House

Edward St. · Dundas St. W. · Dundas Square · Dundas St. E.

Eaton Centre

Mackenzie House

City Hall

Osgoode Hall

Old City Hall

St. Michael's Cathedral

Metro United Church

Nathan Phillips Sq. · Queen St. W. · Queen St. E.

Richmond St. · Adelaide St. · King St. W. · Oxley St. · Peter St. · Widmer St. · John St. · Duncan St. · Simcoe St. · University Ave. · York St. · Bay St. · Victoria St.

Simpsons

Temperance St.

Royal Alexandra Theatre

First Canadian Place

St. James Cathedral

King Edward Hotel

St. Lawrence Hall

Presbyterian Church

Metropolitan Church

Toronto-Dominion Centre

Royal York Hotel

O'Keefe Centre

Royal Bank Plaza

St. Lawrence Market

St. Lawrence Centre

Wellington St. · Clarence Square · Front St. W. · Front St. E.

Union Station

Metro Toronto Convention Centre

N

CN Tower

500 m · 500 yards

Portland St. · Spadina Ave. · York St. · Bay St. · Yonge St. · Lake Shore Blvd.

Redpath Sugar Museum

Lake Shore Blvd. · Gardiner Expressway · Queen's Quay W. · Queen's Quay E.

HAMILTON · OSHAWA

Harbourfront

Loyalism which marked the 1960s are forgotten, and Toronto has become a vibrant city whose colours are displayed in the murals which adorn its streets. Ray Bradbury called it the most perfect city of the western hemisphere—science fiction made real perhaps?

The City

The towers of the financial centre bear witness to Toronto's economic predominance. Walk, or take the red-and-white trolley buses plying to and fro. The Toronto Stock Exchange on York Street provides a good image of this flourishing city. In nearby Bay Street, the sculpted cows by Joe Favard stand as a reminder to economists of every hue that Canada's prosperity reposes on agriculture. In Nathan Philips Square (transformed into a skating rink in winter), the two curved towers of the New City Hall and the Liberty Arches introduce a touch of imagination into the rather staid centre. The grand neo-Gothic Old City Hall, embellished with clock tower and gargoyles, has been converted into a courthouse.

Underground, a veritable warren of galleries linking more than a thousand shops, not to mention cafés, restaurants and cinemas, provides shelter in the winter and air-conditioned relief in summer.

Yonge Street is the main shopping thoroughfare of Toronto, and in fact if you follow it and just keep on walking straight ahead, you will finally reach the Ontario border with Minnesota: it holds the record as the world's longest designated street, 1,896 km (1,178 miles).

Pantages Theatre has been showing *The Phantom of the Opera* since 1988—with a full house every evening. Toronto has become one of the largest filmmaking centres in the English-speaking world, "the Hollywood of the North".

Chinatown

West of University Avenue, there is something of a village atmosphere in Toronto's busy Chinatown, the third biggest in the world. On the pavements, street traders throng before displays of Chinese cabbage, sugar cane and other exotic goods. Neon signs in Mandarin and Cantonese briefly transport you several thousands of miles away.

The Museums

On Dundas Street West, the Art Gallery of Ontario (ARG) is celebrated for its modern paintings and for its collection of Henry

A show staged at the foot of the CN Tower.

Moore sculptures. The Textiles Museum is also in the neighbourhood. However, most of the galleries are found by going north along University Avenue past the Parliament buildings (end 19th century) and the neo-Gothic University (1859). In the Royal Ontario Museum, the magnificent collection of Chinese art is a reminder of the origins of the city's largest cultural minority. In fact all the great civilizations are represented.

Amateur astronomers can stop off at the McLaughlin Planetarium in the same area. At 327 Bloor Street West, the Bata Shoe Museum has an amazing collection of ballet shoes, court shoes and clogs, some of which date from the 16th century.

The CN Tower

It might not be the most attractive building in the city but it's certainly the highest: the CN Tower is Toronto's landmark. At 553 m (1815 ft and 5 inches!) this outsize TV aerial is currently the highest free-standing structure in the world, and the perfect place to get to know the layout of the city. It attracts 1.5 million visitors each year (which should warn you about the length of the queues). The lift takes 58 seconds to take you to the lower observation deck at 335 m (1,222 ft), where the glass floor might make you feel a bit dizzy. A second lift wafts up to the Space Deck at 447 m (1,465 ft). From either of these platforms, the view extends beyond the mirror of Lake Ontario, a distance of 70 km (45 miles). Down below, the redesigned Harbourfront is a vast complex of cultural and entertainment facilities on land reclaimed from the lake. You will also look down on the Skydome, a gigantic stadium of variable geometry where English Canadians can give free rein to their passion for football and baseball.

In the evening, the revolving restaurant enables you to enjoy the whole panorama and a good dinner at the same time. On the ground floor, various attractions delight young and old alike (Q-ZAR—a laser game, and the Simulator Theatre). The brand-new CyberMind, where you can enter the world of virtual reality, is the first of its kind in Canada.

The Islands

Opposite the city, the Toronto Islands are a few scraps of land inhabited by some 700 people. Car-free, and practically shop-free, too, it is an area where many artists have chosen to live and enjoy the peace, as well as the wonderful view of the city. It's less tranquil in summer when Toronto's citizens come in droves to picnic in the public parks.

CULTURAL NOTES

Acadians

French from the earliest days of Canada's colonization, Acadia included today's provinces of Nova Scotia, Prince Edward Island and part of New Brunswick. For many years, until 1755 and the devastating expulsion of its population, its history ran parallel with the history of New France.

What remains today, two and a half centuries later? In New Brunswick, 35 per cent of the population speaks French. Long the exclusive preserve of English speakers, Parliament now has 17 Acadian deputies out of 58. In 1969, official bilingualism was finally voted in. Relegated for generations to the poor coastal lands where they had no option but to become fishermen, Acadians now have access to the French University of Moncton and to the highest levels of administration. In all, there are 300,000 descendants of Acadian colonists for whom French is their mother tongue.

Amerindians

Everything began with a misunderstanding: they were called "Indians" because Christopher Columbus thought he had reached India. The colonists even spoke of "Savages". This was only the first of a long series of mistakes which led to one of the worst genocides in history.

By the end of the 19th century, the Indian population had fallen so low that it was believed they would be completely wiped out. Amerindians number scarcely more than half a million today, scattered among 500 communities on more than 2,000 reserves. There are 63,000 in Quebec representing ten nations, from the largest, the Mohawks (16,000), to the smallest, the Naskapis (400).

The Indians were denied their rights by the federal government for a long time. The right to vote, for example, was conceded only in 1960 (and 1969 for provincial elections). Through progressive access to education, some Amerindians became lawyers, and in Quebec as elsewhere they instituted legal proceedings and won. They were paid compensation for their lost lands and obtained a certain degree of autonomy, electing their own representatives and having their own police. But in the reserves, there is often little real improvement. Unemployment remains high, reaching 80 per cent in some places. Adopting the white 77 man's way of life and living close to their work means exile and severance from their roots, and the slow but inexorable end of an entire people.

Some are reacting. A significant "autonomist" movement started in the 1970s after the American example of Wounded Knee. In 1990 at Oka near Montreal, the Mohawks became famous for their armed resistance to the forces of order while defending a traditional burial ground against the planned extension of a golf course. There are many who support the same cause. Further north, Crees and Inuits together are fighting to prevent Hydro-Quebec from flooding their lands—the combat is peaceful, but the battle is real.

Canoe

Amerindians used to make canoes from birch or spruce bark cut in a single piece. To seal any holes pierced by the rocks, they employed pine resin, which the women chewed to harden. Without the canoe, it would have been impossible for them to cover the distances separating them from their hunting grounds, to cross lakes and rivers and to move around their lands.

The first Europeans to come to Canada understood this. Adopting the Indian canoe, they set off in their turn to explore the territory. These craft would last for a whole season of trapping, and as they were relatively light, could easily be carried when rapids and waterfalls had to be negotiated. It was better not to take risks—many of these men were not swimmers.

French-Canadian Culture

Quebec's national consciousness awoke suddenly in the 1960s. Their balladeers (chansonniers) began to fill the airwaves with nationalist fervour and to throw off the yoke of religion. Félix Leclerc, Gilles Vigneau, Robert Charlebois and Diane Dufresne were leading exponents of the art.

In the theatre, the transition was more painful. Quebec's citizens could not adapt to new plays in joual, the local dialect. Michel Tremblay, however, had an international success with Les Belles-Sœurs, since reconfirmed. After the shock of the failed referendum of 1980, Quebec's artists have turned to the rest of the world. Films by Denys Arcand (Le déclin de l'Empire américain and Jésus de Montréal), the novels of Roger Lémelin (Les Plouffe), of Anne Hébert (Les Fous de Bassan), and of Antonine Maillet (Pélagie la Charrette) have helped to make known abroad—

especially in France—the vigour of Quebec's cultural life. More recent artists are Yves Beauchemin and Jacques Godbout, exposing the bicultural divide, Jacques Poulain and Denise Bombardier and her *Enfance à l'eau bénite*.

Theatre in Quebec Province is among the liveliest in the French-speaking world, with theatre festivals (130 repertory companies), dance, music and comedy all represented.

Trappers

Canada's history begins with the *coureurs des bois*. Hardly had they set foot on dry land than the "wood-runners" set off into the forest in search of what was to become New France's most important export: furs. From the Amerindians they learned how to survive the icy winters, to cope with immense distances and to ignore time. By canoe, sledge and on foot, they traversed the New World. Nothing stopped them, not animals, not tribes on the warpath, not the wearying work.

Many never came back, swallowed up by the vast spaces and the blizzards—or perhaps finding a happier life with the Indians, married to a squaw. Others have described their wanderings, which took them at times as far as the borders of Oregon and Louisiana, and paved the way for the explorers. Today, few maintain the old ways and the number of professional trappers in all Canada is put at about 4,000. In keeping with modern life, they now often travel by snowmobile or amphibious aircraft to inspect their traps.

Maple Syrup

It only takes a few days for spring to awaken. The ground thaws and the sap accumulated all winter in the roots rises in the maple trunks. Once again the syrup season has arrived; in the log cabins of the maple groves, things are on the move.

It was the Amerindians who taught the French colonists how to harvest the juice of the maple. The Indians drank it as it was collected, or boiled it down to make syrup. The amber liquid, traditionally allowed to trickle into jars, but more recently collected by probe and vacuum pump, is heated in the open air, in a huge cauldron. Friends and visitors all join in the "sugaring off": it's a good excuse to celebrate the return of the sun! Traditional treats include eggs thrown into the boiling liquid, and hot syrup dropped on the snow to crystallize then rolled up around a stick—simply scrumptious!

Shopping

Prices in Quebec, although slightly higher than elsewhere in Canada, remain reasonable for Europeans. Shopaholics will have a wonderful time in the large towns, where the malls are always crowded with customers.

Clothing

In general clothing is a good buy. In Montreal, whether you are looking for something classic (designer stores in Sherbrooke Street) or more modern (avant-garde in Boulevard Saint-Laurent, out-of-the-ordinary trendy in Rue Saint-Denis), prices are always affordable. On the Gaspé Peninsula, try something different. The fish-leather clothing to be found at Bonaventure is soft, very hard-wearing and more attractive than you can imagine.

Antiques

Over here, the word "antique" is often used to describe something dating from the time of your grandparents, or even your parents. However, the antique dealers of the Lower Town in Quebec have some handsome Quebecois furniture and silverware. Montreal has a reputation for English porcelain. Art galleries are legion, particularly in Montreal's Sherbrooke Street and Quebec's Rue du Trésor.

Indian Handicrafts

Inuit skills are represented by whalebone, soapstone (steatite) and walrus ivory sculpture. The Crees and Hurons make moccasins, boots and jackets out of caribou skins—some with bead decoration—fur parkas, snowshoes, and the like. Amerindian objects are expensive, but you should bear in mind that they are often the only source of income for the craftsman who made them.

Local Delicacies

It is difficult to resist the maple syrup. That produced in Quebec is quite cheap and of better quality than any other. You will also find all the derivative products: maple sugar, confectionery, and so on.

Or why not take home a lobster fresh from the waters of the Gulf? In Montreal, La Reine de la Mer in Boulevard René-Lévesque packages them and guarantees that they will arrive alive—a definitely different gift.

Dining Out

Quebec may be part of America, but not when it comes to dining out. Even if they are sometimes overwhelmed by fast food from south of the border, the Quebecois still appreciate good eating. The restaurants reflect the province's history, and regional specialities harking back to the diverse origins of the colonists have not been forgotten. Intended to satisfy a trapper's hearty appetite, Quebec's cuisine may seem at first to lack refinement. However, it works wonders with local produce such as salmon, lobster, freshwater fish, game (including caribou), and apples. At the same time, thanks to immigration, all parts of the world are represented gastronomically—Greece, Asia, Portugal…

Breakfast

From first thing in the morning, Quebec's *déjeuners* are intended to keep you going. The "trapper" menu includes eggs, sausages, *cretons* (a sort of potted pork), and beans with bacon. For something a little lighter, try buckwheat pancakes, scrambled eggs with maple syrup and "log-cabin" ham—also with maple syrup.

But nowadays, that, it must be admitted, is the exception rather than the rule. Quebecois serve the traditional American breakfast of fried eggs with bacon or sausages, toast, fruit juice and coffee, generally not very strong—still plenty to keep you going until lunchtime. You can also have cereals, muffins or spongy little pancakes, delicious with maple syrup. Bakeries sell croissants and other pastries of all kinds.

Starters

Traditional Canadian dishes hark back to French country cooking of the past—with some local touches: lamb or kid rillettes *à la charlevoise* accompanied by beetroot jelly and *canneberges* (cranberries); salad with goat's cheese roasted with basil; *confit* of hare; garlic snails in flaky pastry; *cretons* with onion marmalade, etc.

Soups (*potage*) are very popular with the Quebecois, including pea soup with ham and onions, *gourganes* (large red beans), chopped vegetable soup (something like Russian borscht), a delicious turnip and potato soup, and onion soup.

Main dishes

Besides the jugged hare *(civet)*, smoked pheasant, black pudding with apples, pâtés and frogs legs which seem to have come straight from a book of French regional cooking, there are dishes which have disappeared across the Atlantic and yet others which are local inventions. For example, beans with bacon; meat pies *(tourtières)* of hare, pork and caribou; Ile d'Orléans chicken with bacon and apples, anointed with fresh cream and cognac; bacon or ham with caramelized maple sugar; *cipate*, a pâté of mixed meats; *qiaude*, bacon mixed with cod; and *chaudrée*, a kind of hotpot which seems to incorporate whatever ingredients are to hand.

Meats are represented essentially by American beef and more traditionally by lamb (from Charlevoix or the salt meadows of Ile Verte). A reminder of British occupation is roast lamb with sherry and mint sauce—something the French themselves have never been able to appreciate.

Another Quebecois speciality is *poutine*—nothing very exotic. It's a plate of chips sprinkled with cheese curds and drowned in barbecue sauce.

Fish and seafood

Its sea coast and rivers make of Quebec a paradise for lovers of fish. Among the best are the smoked salmon, sturgeon and Ile Verte herring, eels from the lower Saint Lawrence, fillets of sole *en paupiettes* served with a shrimp mousse, fillet of walleye *(doré)* in butter sauce, a speciality from the Ile aux Coudres. *Gibelotte*, popular in the Montérégie region, is a fish soup, similar to French bouillabaisse.

The Magdalen Islands are the ideal place for a lobster diet—they even offer lobsterburgers. Seal also appears on the menu, together with snow crab. Among the shellfish, it's worth tasting the scallops *(pétoncles)* stewed with beans and tarragon.

Amerindian specialities

At the Huron village or in the reserves, you may have the opportunity to taste some Amerindian dishes: bison stew, *sagamité* (corn soup), skewered caribou, *banic* (corn bread with maple syrup), *pemmican* (dried elk meat).

Cheeses and Desserts

There are plenty of cheeses to choose from; the local cheddars are good—try the tasty Oka cheese, the blue Ermite or the Italian-style ricotta, made by Benedictine monks.

In winter, you get to roll your own maple syrup lollipop.

The best desserts are tarts: sugar tart made from maple sugar, cream and walnuts; bilberry pie, sometimes with extra bilberry *coulis* as well; rhubarb or chocolate fudge tart, the addictively delicious butter tart, and the unusual *tarte aux nonnettes*, an ancient recipe from Normandy, with bacon and apples spiced with cinnamon, cloves and nutmeg.

You will find fritters, pancakes and *crèmes caramel*, inevitably laced with maple syrup, and, in summer, freshly picked fruits, including bilberries in August and strawberries and raspberries from the Ile d'Orléans.

Drinks

Wines are mostly imported. French wine is rather expensive, but you can try the very good Californian wines or even the drinkable Chilean and Argentinian wines, on sale everywhere. Quebec produces some wine in the Eastern Townships (whites are best). Many restaurants allow you to bring your own bottle.

Beer is light. There are many makes (Labatt, O'Keefe, Molson...). Cider is also produced locally, and, as a curiosity, you might like to taste bilberry wine (to be drunk chilled), or *caribou*, an explosive mixture of red wine and spirits.

Sports

Water Sports

Water, water everywhere… Rafting, canoeing and kayaking count among the most popular sports, and Quebec's rivers are particularly well adapted to these pastimes. Shooting the Lachine Rapids on the Saint Lawrence is one of the less dangerous trips. More demanding, the descent of the Outaouais River from the Ile du Grand Calumet takes two days.

Swimming is best kept for the gulf, even if the water is a bit chilly. The Saint Lawrence is too polluted for swimming, except at Montreal beach where the water is filtered. You can also sail there. Water sports are paramount in the Outaouais region (Lake Deschênes, Rideau Canal), but not very popular on the river where the currents are too strong.

For the same reason and also because visibility is poor, diving can be risky for beginners. One of the favourite sites among experienced divers is the wreck of the ferry *Empress of Ireland*. Less dangerous, the waters of the gulf are also clearer. There is diving from the Mingan Islands, the Gaspé Peninsula and the Magdalen Islands, celebrated for their caves, their many wrecks—and their lobsters. It is a paradise for windsurfers. Kayaking is practised all along the gulf coast.

Summer Sports

There's no excuse for not getting any excercise. There are countless hiking tracks in Canada, where the wide open spaces are never far away. In the parks, itineraries are marked out, ranging from a few hundred metres to several kilometres.

The Torngat Mountains in the Far North and the Chic-Chocs on the Gaspé Peninsula are the ultimate destinations for the serious trekker. Climbing is also popular, as is hang-gliding: Mont Saint-Pierre on the Gaspé Peninsula is a favourite spot as the winds permit long flights over the gulf.

Horseback riders can hire mounts by the hour or by the day, just about everywhere.

Cycle tracks *(piste cyclable)* are numerous. In Montreal alone there are more than 250 km (150 miles) of cycle paths. There is one leading west along the Saint Lawrence, a favourite for cyclists —and rollerbladers, too. Another pleasant place to cycle is on the Saint Lawrence Islands. Mountain bikes *(vélo de montagne)* are great for getting around the parks.

One man and his dog, waiting for a bite. It's hard to resist the call of the great outdoors, even at sub-zero temperatures!

Golfers are spoilt for choice (but only in summer!). The greatest number of courses is to be found in the Eastern Townships area.

Winter Sports

The Quebecois don't stay indoors in winter. Every hill and hillock in this realm of snow is good for skiing, beginning in November and ending in May. Some of the pistes are illuminated at night: skiing in the dark is more difficult but it can be fun. The landscapes of Mont Tremblant Park in the Laurentians are particularly appreciated by cross-country skiers, as are the Outaouais region and

the Far North. You can even ski in summer on Tadoussac's sand dunes.

The classic method of getting around in winter is by snowshoe *(raquettes)*. It takes some time to learn the right technique and feel completely comfortable shuffling along. If you do venture to the Far North, or even to the Yukon, you can try travelling by dog sled. In Quebec it's more usual to go by snowmobile. There are almost 30,000 km (20,000 miles) of maintained trails. The only drawback, but a considerable one, is the deafening roar of the engine.

If you stay in town, join in the national pastime—ice skating.

Every large community has its own rink. The immense Forum de Montréal has room for 2,000 skaters and 16,000 spectators, so you don't really feel conspicuous even if you're a beginner. In the open air, one of the favourite places for skating is Beaver Lake in Mont Royal Park.

One thing you must not miss is an ice-hockey match. The season lasts from October to April. Canadians throw so much into the sport that they have come to believe they invented it.

Hunting and Fishing

Anglers, fly-fishers, trollers all find paradise in Quebec's tumultuous rivers and thousands of lonely lakes! If you dream of a 190-kg sturgeon at the end of your line (that's the record to date), then you've come to the right place. Walleye and sauger, trout, *ouananiche* (land-locked salmon), Atlantic salmon, Arctic char, trout (red, brown, speckled and rainbow), pickerel, all reach uncommonly large proportions. The muskellunge, a large pike, can reach 20 kg (44 lb). If you prefer sea-fishing, then you can pursue cod, mackerel and even shark off the Magdalen Islands.

In winter, follow the example of the Amerindians and cut a hole in the ice. You will need plenty of patience, and results are not guaranteed. The Canadians often rent fishing huts built over the frozen lakes, complete with a hole in the floorboards!

Hunting is very popular in Quebec and is common everywhere, particularly north of the Saint Lawrence. The favourite prey are the elk (which can weigh up to 600 kg, or 1,300 lb), caribou and deer. During the migratory season, hunting of geese and duck is permitted under strict conditions. For more information on licences, safety regulations, and so on, write to the Ministère du Loisir. de la Chasse et de la Pêche du Québec, Direction des Communications, 150 bvd Saint-Cyrille E, Quebec G1R 4Y1. You can write in English.

SNOW IN MONTREAL

Each winter, Montreal is blanketed by about 2.5 m (8 ft) of snow. With some 1,900 km (1,200 miles) of streets and twice that length of pavement, the city needs 1,400 snow-ploughs to clear it all away.

The operation is expensive (more than $50 million), but the biggest problem is how to dispose of all that snow. Contaminated by exhaust gases and abrasive products, it is too polluted to be simply emptied into the Saint Lawrence. The solution: they incinerate it.

The Hard Facts

To plan your trip, here are some of the practical details you should know about Eastern Canada:

Airports

Montreal has two international airports. You will probably land at Méribel some 60 km (37 miles) out of the city, unless you fly via the United States, in which case you will land at Dorval on the Ile de Montréal. Toronto's Pearson International Airport is 30 km (18 miles) outside the city. Quebec and Ottawa also have international airports.

Climate

They say that summer in Quebec begins on July 14 and ends on August 15. Be that as it may, winter certainly dominates the climate. The average temperature in Montreal in January is –10.2°C (13.6°F), but has been known to descend to –35°C (–31°F). Snow starts falling in November and disappears completely only in May. Montreal receives 2.5 m (8 ft) every year and endures eight or ten blizzards (*poudreries*).

Spring is short, followed by a hot—and somewhat rainy—summer. Temperatures can soar to 30°C (86°F) or even 35°C (95°F).

From the end of August the temperatures start to drop. The last fine days are those of the Indian summer at the beginning of October.

Communications

To telephone to Europe, dial 011 followed by the country code (44 for the UK), then the area code minus the initial zero and the local number. If you are using a public telephone box, have a large reserve of 25¢ coins. The operator will ask you to pay in advance for a three-minute call and will request further payment if you stay on line for longer than that. Quebec has recently adopted the use of phone cards (Allô), which are easier and cheaper to use. If you wish to make a reverse charge call (*renverser les charges*), announce this to the operator. Calls from hotels are always more expensive.

The use of fax machines is common and every hotel will send them for you for a fixed price. Post takes 4 to 7 days to reach a European destination, longer for postcards.

Currency

The monetary unit of Canada is the Canadian dollar (C$), divided into 100 cents. There are banknotes of 5, 10, 20, 50, 100 and 1,000 dollars and coins of 1, 5, 10, and 25 cents and 1 and 2 dollars. The Quebecois frequently refer to *piastres* ($) and *sous* (¢).

Credit cards are accepted almost everywhere, Mastercard being preferred. After that, in order of preference, Visa, American Express and Diners Club.

If you know your PIN number, then you can withdraw money from cash dispensers (again, preponderantly Mastercard). Traveller's cheques in Canadian dollars are accepted in all shops, hotels and restaurants like cash. They even give change.

Driving

Roads are good, especially when you consider the climatic conditions. Motorways (no charge) follow the main routes east-west. Canadians drive a lot and distances mean little to them. Perhaps this is in part because petrol is cheap (the price varies from province to province).

All speed limits are posted in kilometres per hour. Keep within the limits or be prepared to pay the fine: 100 kph (60 mph) on the motorway, 90 kph (55 mph) on major roads, 70 kph (40 mph) on minor roads and 50 kph (30 mph) in town. Distances are also marked in kilometres; to work out the equivalent in miles, multiply by 5 and divide by 8.

Parking rules are strictly enforced in the city centres by efficient traffic wardens who patrol the streets. Offending vehicles are towed away. It's best to pay for a car park.

Drive on the right, and keep your seatbelt fastened: heavy fines are imposed on those who ignore the rules. Turning right on a red light is strictly prohibited in Quebec, unless there's an additional green arrow indicating that you *can* turn right. Watch out for yellow school buses. Stationary buses with their red lights flashing means that children are getting off or on and cars must stop; on no account can you overtake.

Electricity

All electrical installations are 110 volts AC, 60 Hz. Electrical outlets are of the American type, with sockets for two flat pins. If you are thinking of using electrical equipment (hairdryer, electric razor or personal computer), take an adaptor or even a transformer.

Emergencies

One single telephone number for every type of emergency—**911**. The operator contacts the required service for you: fire, police or ambulance.

Essentials

Anything which you may have forgotten is obtainable here. However, if you are following a course of medical treatment, then bring your prescription drugs with you, as brands and dosage vary.

For summer, light clothing is advisable, with a sweater for the evenings and a raincoat for wet days. In winter, dress as if you were going skiing—and remember that it will be colder than that.

Formalities

British citizens do not need a visa to enter Canada but they must have a valid passport. American citizens need proof of citizenship such as birth certificate or a voter's registration card.

You may need to produce a return or onward ticket. Customs regulations forbid the importation of foodstuffs of animal or vegetable origin.

Anyone over 16 may import 200 cigarettes and 50 cigars; anyone over 18 is allowed to bring 1.1 litres of wine or spirits, or 8.5 litres of beer.

Health

Medical care, particularly hospital treatment, is very expensive. Find out if your health insurance at home extends to hospital or doctor visits overseas. If not, take out a medical insurance against all costs incurred abroad, including repatriation.

During warm weather, watch out for insect bites. Myriads of vicious mosquitoes and blackflies hatch out at the same time and you can collect dozens of bites in one day, which can make life a misery. Cover yourself from head to foot and douse yourself with insect repellent.

Language

Quebec is French-speaking and proud of it. The English-speaking population is essentially found in Montreal and represents only 15 per cent of the 6.5 million inhabitants. For the Quebecois, their language is the focus of their cultural struggle. The local dialect, called *Joual*, has adopted words from all sources: old French, Americanisms, Amerindian words, English vocabulary and literal translations from English that are highly amusing to the French. The accent is rustic and sing-song, gives a unique, colourful flavour to Quebec French, unlike anything you may have learnt at school. Do not be surprised if you are addressed in the familiar "tu" form.

This said, there is no need to worry if you only speak English. Whereas many French speakers of the older generation do not (and will not) understand English, it is spoken by practically all of the younger generation. In Ontario and Toronto in particular, French is dying out.

Media

In Quebec, the market is dominated by three French daily papers. *La Presse* (highest circulation), *Le Journal de Montréal* (the most popular) and *Le Devoir* (the most highbrow). The weekly *Voir* is a good source of information about the cultural scene. There is one English language paper published in Montreal, *The Gazette*, which is anti-separatist. All the major international English newspapers and magazines are available.

Radio and television broadcasts are in both French and English (CTV and CBC). Specialized coverage is very extensive: RDI, the information network, RDS, the sports network, Météo Média for the weather, Canal Famille, the family channel, Télé Immeubles for illustrated small ads, and even a horoscope channel. In addition, there are hundreds of cable channels. In the south of Quebec and in Ontario, several American channels can be received.

National Parks

The first National Park was designated in 1887 by the Canadian government, to limit the damage done by trapping. Today there are 31 distributed across the country. Whether they are nature parks or historic parks, each has a reception centre and an interpretive centre where you can familiarize yourself with local conditions. Very well worthwhile for information on the fauna, hiking trails, etc.

Opening Hours

Small shops are usually open Monday to Wednesday from 9 a.m. to 6 p.m., Thursday and Friday to 9 p.m. They are also open on Saturdays from 9 a.m. to 5 p.m. and sometimes on Sundays from 11 a.m. to 5 p.m. Large stores operate on the American model, closing between 8 p.m. and 10 p.m. Corner grocery stores usually stay open every day from 7 a.m. until 10 p.m.

Banks are open continuously Monday to Friday from 10 a.m. until 4 p.m. except on Thursdays when they close at 8 p.m.

Many museums and attractions reduce their opening hours or even close completely from the month of September.

Photography

All existing film types are available. You can also have your photographs developed on the spot. Charges are lower than in Europe and virtually every shop has a one-hour service. This is not the case, however, for slides or black-and-white film, not very common in North America.

Public holidays

Banks and offices are closed on the following days:

January 1	New Year
March-April	Good Friday
	Easter Monday
3rd Monday in May	Dollard Day
June 24	Quebec National Day
July 1	Confederation Day
1st Monday in September	Labour Day
2nd Monday in October	Action de Grâce (Thanksgiving)
Dec. 25–26	Christmas

Religion

Not so long ago, Quebec was staunchly Catholic. Their faith helped the French speakers to maintain for their identity in the face of English Protestantism. Until the 1960s, religion governed everything, even work. During a visit at the end of the 19th century, Mark Twain wrote "if you throw a brick from any street corner in Montreal, you are sure to break a church window".

Safety

Canada is a safe country and the crime rate is very low. In Mon-treal or Toronto you can use the metro late at night without fear.

In the parks, never leave food close to your car or your tent. Bears are never very far away, and attracted by the smell, could try to help themselves. Do as hikers do, and use a rope to hang your groceries from a tree.

Tax Rebates

Purchases costing more than $50 and destined for export, as well as hotel bills for non-residents of Canada, can benefit from tax rebates. You have to make the request in a duty-free shop, at the airport when you leave, or at the frontier if you are crossing into the United States. Remember to keep your original receipts. It is possible to be reimbursed by post. For further details, consult the government brochure, available in tourist offices, hotels and some shops.

Time Difference

Quebec and Ontario keep the same time, GMT –5. When it is noon in London, it is 7 a.m. in Montreal or Toronto. Canada observes summer time, which is GMT –4.

Tipping

In bars and restaurants, service is never included. Reckon on 10 to 15 per cent of the total bill, excluding the tax. Taxi drivers, bellboys and hairdressers are tipped at the customer's discretion. There is no tipping in theatres and cinemas.

Toilets

Public toilets are found at airports, railway and bus stations, in the large stores and petrol stations. Restaurants keep theirs for customers only.

Tourist Offices

Quebec is divided into sixteen tourist regions and each has its own tourist office with both permanent and temporary local branches (open from June until October along the main roads), all competent and providing excellent, informative brochures. You can also dial the toll-free number 1 800 363 7777 to obtain information on sporting and cultural events, hotels, restaurants, and so on.

Transport

Air travel is the only option for long distances. Numerous airlines provide flights to an improbable number of destinations. Air Canada and Canadian Airlines both offer a pass which is valid for their entire network (this must be bought in Europe). More locally, and especially in the north, amphibious aircraft provide breathtaking flights across Quebec's forest. One serious inconvenience is that flights are expensive in Canada.

You can travel by train from the Atlantic to the Pacific. From Montreal to Vancouver takes over three days at an average speed of 60 kph (37 mph). The fixed-price Canrail Pass allows unlimited travel for a month.

You can also travel from one end of Quebec (and even of Canada) to the other by long-distance bus. There are passes for the national Greyhound service or the Quebec and Ontario Voyageur service which are valid for 30 and 20 days respectively.

For shorter distances, and for the freedom it gives, there is no better solution than hiring a car (see also under DRIVING). All the major car hire companies are represented, and you can pay for the rental at the same time as your air fare (fly-drive). Charges are relatively competitive and usually include 1,000 to 1,200 km (625 to 750 miles) per week. There is no unlimited mileage rental. Another possibility is to hire a car in the United States and drive it across the border. It is absolutely legal, and works out much cheaper if long distances are involved. In either case, the minimum age is 25, occasionally less but then always over 21 and with a heavy extra daily charge. European driving licences are recognized, as is the international licence.

As an alternative to a car, try renting a camping-car, which in addition will solvem, all your accommodation problems. They have all modern conveniences aboard: hot water, shower, kitchenette, etc. In summer, you have to reserve in advance.

Local public transport is efficient and cheap. Bus and trolley routes cover the larger towns with regular services. You must have the exact change for the driver.

Montreal and Toronto also have metro services which are fast, clean and safe and very practical.

Taxis are numerous and very reasonably priced. In Montreal you can hail them on the street; everywhere else in Quebec you have to call by phone or go to the taxi ranks at airports, train and bus stations and outside the major hotels. Fares are based on the number of kilometres clocked up on the meter.

Labrador Coast

The Big Land

Labrador has hardly changed in millions of years. The air is crisp and pure, the rivers icily transparent, the lakes teeming with trout, the mountains and icebergs silhouetted razor sharp against the clear blue sky. Most nights, the Aurora Borealis unfolds its shimmering curtain of light and colour. To Labrador's indigenous peoples, the Innu and Inuit, the Northern Lights were the spirits of the dead, dancing and waving in the sky.

A great wedge of land bordering Quebec, Labrador is part of the Canadian province of Newfoundland (officially called Newfoundland and Labrador), covering 300,000 sq km (112,000 sq miles). Most of it is wilderness, roamed by moose, black bears, wolves, lynx, porcupine and the world's largest barren-land caribou herd (450,000-strong). Of the 30,000 hardy inhabitants, more than half live in four towns, all built in the mid-20th century: Labrador City and adjoining Wabush, Churchill Falls and Happy Valley-Goose Bay. The rest are scattered along the coast in tiny fishing villages. The coastal population is largely made up of native peoples and descendants of the European settlers that came here to make a living from whaling and trapping. Because of their relative isolation from the rest of the world, all these peoples have nurtured their ancient traditions.

The Trans Labrador Highway, Route 500, slashes across the region, linking Labrador City, on the border with Quebec, to Happy Valley and Goose Bay at the end of the Hamilton Inlet—a fairly rough 9-hour trip. The communities along the southeast coast, from Blanc Sablon in Quebec to Red Bay, are served by an 80-km stretch of paved highway, Route 510. Other towns along the coast, as far north as Nain, can be reached by boat or plane, while the more northerly fjords and mountain ranges and the challenging interior are accessible only by private plane. Increasing numbers of adventurous visitors hire a seaplane pilot to take them to some remote lake with a canoe and supplies and arrange to be picked up a week or so later.

Hotel accommodation is developing, but many people prefer camping. Predictably, there are plenty of activities for outdoors enthusiasts, including world-class fishing, whitewater canoeing, hiking along the trappers' trails (known as traplines), skiing and dog-sledding. The less energetic come to cheer the famous 6-day Labrador 400 International Sled Dog Race, which takes place every year in March, or to go whalewatching or iceberg-spotting off the coast.

A Brief History

Early times	Around 7000 BC, Aboriginal peoples settle on the southeast coast. A thousand years later, Maritime Archaic Indian peoples migrate to Labrador and live from fishing, hunting and gathering berries and plants. Eskimos appear around 2000 BC, followed by other groups including the Inuit.
11th century	Viking trader Bjarni Herjolfson and his crew are blown off course on their way to a Norse colony in Greenland and reach Labrador around the year 1000. They take one look and sail off south to Newfoundland where they settle at L'Anse aux Meadows on the island's tip.
16th–17th centuries	Parts of the coast are explored by Gaspar Corte-Real, Jacques Cartier, Martin Frobisher and others. The name Labrador is derived from one of the names bestowed on the region, *Tierra del Labrador* (Land of the Working Man, in Spanish). Basques and other Europeans settle on the coast to hunt for whales and produce whale oil.
18th–19th centuries	Labrador remains undefined geographically until 1763 when the Treaty of Paris assigns it to Great Britain. The Hudson's Bay Company establishes a post on the Hamilton Inlet to trade with the native peoples. Fur trappers explore central Labrador. Fishermen from Newfoundland settle along Labrador's southeast coast, north of the Strait of Belle Isle, and Labrador is made a dependency of Newfoundland. Moravian missionaries arrive in 1771 from Germany, establishing a settlement at Nain. Expansion of the fisheries leads to the creation of permanent settlements at Battle Harbour, Goose Bay, Nain and Hopedale. Labrador is transferred to Quebec in 1774 and returned to Newfoundland in 1809.
20th century	During the early 1930s, mining companies begin to secure concession rights in Labrador and Quebec. Labrador City and Wabush are built around the iron ore mining industry. The western hemisphere's largest hydroelectric generator is built in Churchill Falls, supplying more than half the electricity used by Quebec and northeast USA. During World War II a major airfield is built at Goose Bay, strategically sited on the air route between USA and Europe. Today it serves as a supply centre and an installation for low-level flight training by several NATO forces.

97

Sightseeing

A tour of Labrador's coast begins at **St Barbe** on Newfoundland's northern peninsula, linked by ferry to **Blanc Sablon** on the Quebec-Labrador boundary. The Strait of Belle Isle, dividing the two land-masses, is only 18 km (11 miles) wide at this point; during late spring and early summer, melting icebergs float along this "Iceberg Alley", carried by the Labrador Current from Greenland to the warmer waters of the St Lawrence where they eventually break up.

Forteau, the largest of the area's half-dozen permanent communities, hosts an annual, four-day August Bakeapple Folk Festival of music, dance, storytelling and crafts. Between Forteau and L'Anse-au-Loup, visit the **Labrador Straits Regional Museum**, displaying regional artefacts including an old sleigh, or *komatik*.

At **L'Anse-Amour**, a mound of stones marks the burial place of a Maritime Archaic Indian child, dating back some 7,500 years. This is the earliest known funeral monument of the New World. Various artefacts such as a harpoon head and bone whistle were found with the body.

To take in the sweeping views of the ocean, stop at the **Point Amour lighthouse** and climb its 122 steps to the light-room.

Despite its powerful beam, many ships have run aground off this particularly hazardous stretch of coastline, prone to fog, snowstorms, icebergs and dangerous currents, not to mention hidden rocks.

In the late 1970s, underwater archaeologists discovered the remains of three 16th-century Basque whaling ships sunk in **Red Bay**'s harbour, while land excavations disclosed more than twenty refineries where the whales were processed and their blubber rendered into precious oil. Whaling artefacts such as iron harpoons, 16th-century seaman's clothing and coopers' tools are displayed in the Visitor Centre. You can take a boat shuttle to neighbouring **Saddle Island** where 140 skeletons have been unearthed from the whalers' cemetery.

The road ends here and the only ways of progressing further north is by coastal boat or plane. The boat from Lewisporte on Newfoundland island to Nain takes two weeks for the return trip, stopping at every isolated community along the rugged coast to load and unload supplies. A car ferry links Lewisporte to Cartwright and Happy Valley-Goose Bay, a 33-hour journey one way.

Cut off from the mainland by a stretch of water called the

The Point Amour lighthouse helped European vessels to reach their Canadian destination in safety.

"tickle", **Battle Harbour** is one of the oldest settlements of the coast, fished since 1759. Abandoned by all but seasonal fishermen in the 1960s, this home of Labrador's first telegraph station, hospital, lighthouse and Anglican church—now a cluster of square wooden buildings nestling beneath a rugged cliff — has been restored as a historic site.

Port Hope Simpson and **Charlottetown**, in a heavily forested region, are 20th-century settlements, founded for the timber industry.

Cartwright was named after a merchant adventurer who lived on the coast at the end of the 18th century. His house is marked by a big boulder known as Caribou Castle. Today the community is an important service centre for fishermen. You can buy a crab at the processing plant. Campers are not deterred by the black bears and caribou that sometimes wander down to the 56-km (36-mile) stretch of sand known as **Porcupine Strand**, just outside Cartwright; legend has it that the Vikings called this beach "Wonderstrands".

99

The recognition of Battle Harbour's historical importance has brought new life to its craggy shores.

Rigolet, at the entrance of the deep Hamilton Inlet, was founded in 1787 as a fur trading centre. The Hudson's Bay Company has operated a trading post here since 1837; modern life has bypassed the community except for a short period during World War II when it was the site of a Canadian army base.

At the end of the Trans Labrador Highway, **Happy Valley-Goose Bay**, with a population of 8,600, is one of the region's largest towns. Since World War II it has remained an aviation centre, and low-flying aircraft often zoom overhead. Though the young folk may complain there's nothing much to do in town, things liven up in the winter months when there are endless possibilities for all kinds of unusual snow sports: dog-team riding or skijoring, snowmobiling and snowshoeing, in addition to cross-country and downhill skiing. The Labrador Winter Games are held every three years, and dog team races and the Happy Goose carnival take place in March.

To learn more about the early days, pay a call to the **Labrador**

Heritage Museum, on the former Canadian Forces Base, which documents the land and people by photographs and manuscripts, as well as samples of furs amd minerals. The **Northern Lights Military Museum** on Hamilton River Road depicts the province's military history, while in the same building, the **Trappers Brook Animal Displays** illustrate the varied fauna of the region, from ducks to black bears, including giant brook and lake trout that didn't get away.

Back on the coast, **Makkovik** seems lost in time. A Norwegian fur trader and his Labrador wife founded the community in the early 1800s, and by the end of the century it had expanded enough to merit a church, built by the Moravian missionaries. The Moravians operated from Nain, converting north-coast Inuit to Christianity. By 1900 they had built a chain of settlements, each with school, trading post and church, from Makkovik to Killinek at the very tip of Labrador. Most of these were abandoned as the Inuit moved towards the more "civilized" towns of Nain, Hopedale and Goose Bay. The **Hopedale Mission** (1782) is the oldest wooden frame building east of Quebec and has been preserved as a National Historic Site. The Minister's quarters now serve as the **Agvituk Heritage Museum**, with collections of furniture, books and tools of both Moravian and Inuit communities.

A little town of 1000, **Nain** is the last stop on the boat and ferry routes. The Moravian Mission has been converted into a museum outlining Inuit and Moravian history. Signposted as **Piumlimatsivik** ("the place where we keep old things"), it offers a strange compromise between the well-intentioned German missionaries who tried to wipe out the indigenous religion and the Inuit valiantly striving to keep their language and traditions alive. At the Sunday services in the Moravian church, the congregation sings old German hymns in Inuktitut.

Eating Out

Labrador brings another meaning to the term "Eating Out". Back to nature is the theme of any visit to this wild and remote region, and part of the entertainment is the traditional "boil up": keeping your hands warm round a cup of hot tea while your dinner cooks over an open fire. Anything seems good for a boil up: freshly fished trout or Arctic char, ptarmigan or caribou, clams and mussels dug up from Cartwright's beach, crab in Mary's Harbour. And dessert can be gathered from the bushes: tangy bakeapples, also known as cloudberries, a 101 lumpy-looking golden fruit that grows in profusion in southern Labrador and is considered a great delicacy.

Shopping

Every community in Labrador has its little craft shop where you'll find a wide selection of beautifully produced articles tracing the traditions of whalers, Inuit and Innu peoples. Hooked rugs, quilts, soapstone carvings, knitted items, snowshoes, Innu tea dolls, labradorite jewellery, sealskin mittens, moose-hide slippers, antler buttons and objects made from grass are just a few examples of the fine native arts.

Practical Information

Currency. The Canadian dollar is divided into 100 cents. Notes: $5 to $1,000. Coins: 1¢ to $2.

Telephone. Labrador (area code 709) is part of the US network. To call the UK, dial 011 44, the area code minus the initial zero, and the local number.

Newfoundland

Vikings and Brits

This island fastness lies just off the Labrador coast, between the Gulf of St Lawrence and the chill North Atlantic. It's more like two islands, really, a large one joined by an isthmus to the smaller Avalon Peninsula—site of the capital, St John's, part fishing village, part high-rise city. Together with Labrador, it forms the Canadian province of Newfoundland.

This is a place of forests, lakes and rivers, fringed with fjords, crested with mountains. Rugged, even forbidding, the landscape has a cold, hard, unyielding beauty, honed by wind and water. Here, on the northern reaches of North America, you will marvel at the spectacle of surging surf and wheeling sea birds—petrels, puffins, guillemots and murres. You may catch sight of caribou herds, black bears, whales and schools of dolphin, sea lions, otters—and the odd iceberg drifting south.

One main road bisects the island, the last leg of the Trans Canada Highway. Smaller roads branch off to 1,000 km of coastal scenery, dotted with tiny fishing settlements.

A thousand years ago, Viking seafarers ventured this way. They established a colony in the north of the island, on a site now called L'Anse aux Meadows. But it was only in 1497, with the arrival of the adventurer John Cabot, that this "new found land" received its name and a certain renown—for the rich fishing banks just off shore. English ships came to trawl in Newfoundland waters, and within a century, England had claimed the island as its own. There Newfoundland's loyalties lay—until the island joined the Canadian confederation as the Dominion's 10th province in 1949.

Some 525,000 friendly "Newfies"—sturdy individualists all—live on Newfoundland Island's 112,000 sq km (43,000 sq miles). Largely of English or Irish extraction, they still speak in the accents of the old country, 2,560 km (1,600 miles) or so away. Isolated from Europe and the North American mainland, the islanders developed a culture uniquely their own, and even now the old folk traditions survive, along with a taste for tea, rum and fried cod tongues—rather like clams—and a passion for hunting, fishing and the outdoor life.

Many cruise ships follow the route of the great fishing fleets to historic St John's on the Atlantic, the principal port, sailing on to Corner Brook, gateway to the wildly romantic west coast, sometimes calling in at the French Saint-Pierre et Miquelon. A journey that takes on the thrill of a voyage of discovery.

A Brief History

6th–11th centuries	Irish mariners probably visit Newfoundland. Norsemen found a colony on the north coast, on the site of L'Anse aux Meadows, in about AD 1000.
14th–15th centuries	Basque fishermen trawl the North Atlantic near the Newfoundland coast. English sailors make their way to the island. In 1497, John Cabot, remembered as the "discoverer" of Newfoundland, lands on the east coast.
16th century	Fishermen from England, France, Spain and Portugal come in pursuit of cod. Sir Humphrey Gilbert claims Newfoundland for England in 1583. The peaceful Beothuck Indians retreat to the interior (disappearing by the 19th century).
17th century	English colonies are founded at Cupids (1610) and Ferryland (1622). Affairs are administered locally on a year-to-year basis by the Fishing Admiral—the captain of the first ship to enter harbour in any given season. The island becomes a favoured haunt of pirates. The French establish a settlement at Placentia in 1662. They launch attacks on British ports, occupying St John's in 1696.
18th century	The French take St John's yet again in 1708. They are ousted by the British, who strengthen the fortifications and install a garrison of soldiers. At the conclusion of the War of the Spanish Succession, the Treaty of Utrecht (1713) affirms British sovereignty over Newfoundland, but French rivalry continues. The last serious battle takes place in 1762, at the end of the Seven Years' War, when St John's is occupied by the French for three months. Captain Cook explores the west coast of Newfoundland in 1764.
19th century	Newfoundland becomes a British colony in 1824. When the Canadian confederation is founded, the island maintains its independence. The island becomes an important shipbuilding centre in the 1880s. St John's is ravaged by fire in 1892 and completely rebuilt.
20th century	Guglielmo Marconi receives the first transatlantic wireless message on Signal Hill in St John's in 1901. Many pioneering plane crossings lift off from here. Newfoundland serves as a staging area in the two world wars. Together with Labrador, it joins the Dominion of Canada in 1949. Oil is discovered just off shore.

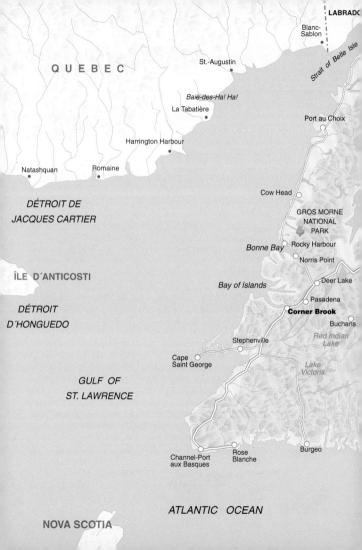

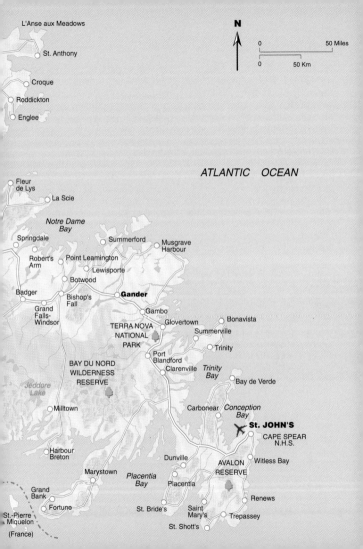

Sightseeing

St Johns

Where better to begin than "Sint Johns" (population 175,000), as the locals say it. They attribute the name to the saint's day of John the Baptist, June 24, when explorer John Cabot arrived there (or somewhere near) in 1497. But be prepared: sensible shoes are a must in this up-and-down, cobblestoned town.

A channel known as the Narrows leads into the spectacular sweep of **St John's Harbour**. The town burned down three times in the 19th century, but each time it has been rebuilt, as today, with gaily painted wooden houses overlooking the waterfront. They make a colourful contrast with the austere grey trawlers all the way from Britain, and often Russia and Japan, too. Ships from around the world tie up by **Harbour Drive**, including the vessels that supply Newfoundland's offshore oil rigs. In the **Murray Premises**, an old fishery warehouse transformed into a shopping centre, is a four-storey annexe to the Newfoundland Museum (see below), tracing the lively seafaring history of the province. Look for the Newfoundland dog marking the entrance.

More shops and small businesses line harbourfront **Water Street**, St John's oldest thoroughfare. Catering to seamen from five continents, the sailors' pubs here have an international reputation. Some of the prettiest Victorian houses, painted rich burgundy, bright yellow or deep amber, are to be found on **New Gower Street** running parallel to the harbour.

On Gower Street, the neo-Gothic **Anglican Cathedral** in Newfoundland bluestone was twice destroyed by fire and twice rebuilt. Take history in your stride as you head down Duckworth Street, with its painted, wood-frame houses and concentration of craft shops. Here is the main building of the **Newfoundland Museum**, displaying rare Beothuck Indian artefacts and colonial relics. The exhibits include the costume, furniture and implements of the first European fishermen.

St John's Roman Catholics claim the town's dominant landmark, the **Basilica of St John the Baptist**, an imposing stone structure of the mid-19th century. From here, Military Road takes you to another cluster of historic institutions: the **Colonial Building**, once seat of the government and now Newfoundland's Provincial Archives; **Government House**, residence of the Lieutenant Governor; the **Old Garrison Church**, officially known as

St Thomas's (1821); and **Commissariat House**, completed the same year. British military officers charged with the administration of the colony of Newfoundland lived in this Georgian-style clapboard house, decorated with period furnishings.

In the old days, townspeople rigged a chain across the harbour entrance for protection from pirates and marauding Frenchmen. A further deterrent was provided by the heavy artillery of the **Queen's Own Battery**, the rambling fortification set high above the Narrows on **Signal Hill**, a National Historic Park. It was here that Marconi received the first transatlantic wireless message, transmitted from Cornwall in England. It came through at precisely 12.30 p.m., December 12, 1901, to a receiving station that the Italian inventor had set up on the hill in a hospital (destroyed by fire in 1920). Marconi suddenly started shouting: "Do you hear that? Do you hear that?" All they could hear—he and a few local fishermen gathered there to listen in—were a repeated series of three faint bips, Morse code for the letter S.

The name of the hill, however, predates that momentous event by several centuries, recalling instead the standard raised above the summit whenever a ship sailed into the harbour. Exhibits in **Cabot Tower**, on the hillside, commemorate Marconi's achiev-

---

NEWFOUNDLAND'S LIFEGUARD

Lassie may be more of a celebrity, with its face plastered in books and films galore, but the Newfie, the down-to-earth, hard-working Newfoundland dog, scorns all that razzle-dazzle show-biz and just gets on with its chores. This is a *serious* dog, with important work to do, like saving drowning sailors or fishermen from the frigid seas. Big (71 cm, or 28 in, at the shoulder), heavy (50–63 kg, or 110–140 lb) and strong, the silky black dog—or sometimes black-and-white—has been responsible for many rescues at sea. Its large feet are webbed, making it the champion swimmer of all dogdom, and a dense double coat of fur wards against the lowest temperatures. The locals praise to the heavens the gentleness, intelligence and loyalty of this excellent guard dog, most likely a cross of the American black wolf and the huge bear dogs brought to the continent by the Vikings. So let Lassie hog the cameras—the Newfie dog is confident of its loftier pedigree and has no need to boast.

ement. The tower itself was put up in 1897, on the 400th anniversary of Cabot's discovery of Newfoundland. Climb to the top for stunning views of the city and nearby Cape Spear, jutting eastwards into the blue immensity of the Atlantic.

Also on Signal Hill, the Visitor Reception and Interpretation Centre screens a film about Newfoundland, past and present. If you're in luck, your visit may coincide with a performance of the Signal Hill Tattoo, a military drill staged in period uniform.

Quidi Vidi (pronounced "Kiddy Viddy") is a fishing village on the far side of Signal Hill. Watch the fishing boats come in, sails aloft, hulls laden with the day's haul of salmon, cod and shellfish. They slip through the Gut, an inlet north of the Narrows, overlooked by the French-built **Quidi Vidi Battery**. The fortification, or what remains of it, is a popular tourist sight: "soldiers" kitted out in period battledress recall old conflicts—from the Seven Years' War with the French to the War of 1812 between Britain and the US. **Quidi Vidi Lake** is the scene of the spectacular St John's Regatta on the first Wednesday in August. Begun in the 1820s, this race for six-oar rowing boats is the oldest continuing sporting event in North America and is also the occasion for an unusually exuberant carnival.

On the outskirts of town to the northwest, the sleekly modern **Arts and Culture Centre** houses an art gallery, theatre, library and small museum. Parliament sits in the **Confederation Building**, further along the road.

North of St John's, **Marine Drive** takes you along the characteristically craggy coast of the Avalon Peninsula through the fishing villages of Outer Cove, Middle Cove and Torbay up to the pretty little Pouch Cove. Look out for the whales that pass down this coast in summer. On the shore, you'll see the wooden trestled racks on which fishermen still dry the cod in the time-honoured manner.

You can't go farther east than **Cape Spear**, 16 km (10 miles) from St John's—unless it's to Ireland, next stop across the Atlantic. The cape is a popular tourist spot: a national historic site focuses on a white clapboard lighthouse built in 1835; it has been nicely renovated with a red and white striped dome, but it's the ugly modern concrete tower that does all the work. You'll also see some ruined World War II gun emplacements, a reminder of the days when German U-boats cruised uncomfortably close to shore.

Continuing south along the coast, you're confronted with nature at its most savage and sublime. Barren headlands plunge into a seething sea, while here and there a fishing village—known as "outposts"—finds a precarious hold on the rocky shore and seabirds soar skywards, braving the buffeting winds. Three islands form an extraordinary bird sanctuary at **Witless Bay**, where puffins, petrels, murres and other seabirds nest and hatch their young. At the tip of the Cape Shore, the southwest arm of the Avalon Peninsula, **Cape St Mary's Ecological Reserve** is one of the largest nesting grounds in North America for gannets. You can walk up close to the birds.

At **Placentia**, founded in 1662 and the former French capital of Newfoundland, see the remains of the old fort at Castle Hill.

East Newfoundland

The area designated as East Newfoundland covers the eastern part of the bigger "island", from Cape Bonavista in the north to the Burin Peninsula in the south.

The town of **Bonavista** claims to be the site where John Cabot first landed, though there is some debate as to whether it was here or at St John's. In a particularly scenic setting, the red-and-white striped lighthouse at the tip of the cape has been restored as a historic site, where guides in period costume show you around the lightkeeper's living quarters as they would have been in the 1870s.

Pretty **Trinity**, established in 1580, is one of the oldest towns in the whole of America. Whale-watching expeditions can be organized from here.

The Trans Canada Highway runs through **Terra Nova National Park**, 240 km (150 miles) from St John's. You can take a boat tour or walk around the estuary of **Newman Sound**. Nature-lovers are intrigued by the abundance of waterfowl—all manner of wild duck, notably the neither-goose-nor-gander goosander, also known locally as merganser—and other marine life ranging from humpback whale to plankton. Paddle around the tidal pools to spot the smaller creatures, nothing nasty to sting you here. The dense boreal forest of spruce and fir throws a rich green blanket over 400 sq km (16,000 acres) of the park, with birch and juniper in the valleys. One of the park's most spectacular panoramas, viewed from **Ochre Hill**, is the stark boulder-strewn landscape created by primeval glaciers. In the spring, you'll see their latter-day offspring, icebergs drifting in from Bonavista Bay, warning off any would-be *Titanic*.

The very name of **Gander** is enough to thrill aviation buffs. The airport, opened in 1938, was a pioneer in transatlantic flight. During World War II it was a major refuelling base. The development of non-stop jetliners left it a backwater, but Gander remains a haven for all kinds of planes in trouble in the North Atlantic looking for a safe landing. An exhibit in the Domestic Passenger's Lounge illustrates Newfoundland's crucial role in the early years of transatlantic flight, while four historic aircraft are displayed on Elizabeth Drive in downtown Gander.

On the Burin Peninsula, **Fortune** is the ferry gateway to Saint-Pierre et Miquelon, a little piece of French civilization just 20 km (12 miles) off the coast.

The West

Corner Brook occupies an impressive site on the Gulf of St Lawrence, at the mouth of the Humber River beneath the peaks of the Long Range Mountains. The town of more than 30,000 has made a graceful transition from fishing village to commercial centre (paper and cement are big business here), with salmon fishing along the Humber, hunting around Deer Lake, 50 km (30 miles) to the east, and skiing just minutes away at Marble Mountain.

ST-PIERRE ET MIQUELON

People here find their *joie de vivre* in fresh croissants, a good bottle of Burgundy or Bordeaux and a cuisine with a refinement that seems a world away from the simpler fare dished up by the big Canadian neighbour. The islands are now a French Territorial Collectivity.

The archipelago has three main islands—with almost 90 per cent of the 6,000 inhabitants living on the smallest, St-Pierre, covering just 12 sq km (5 sq miles). A ferry ride to the northwest, the other two, Grande-Miquelon and Petite-Miquelon, also known as Langlade, are joined by a sandbar (augmented by a landfill of shipwreck timber) and inhabited by a few hundred fishermen and a host of sea birds.

In the town around St Pierre harbour, the main square is Place du Général-de-Gaulle, gendarmes look like gendarmes, the Renaults and Peugeots outnumber the Hondas, and the Catholic church is hybrid French provincial, but the style of the houses is strictly New England clapboard. Some of them are in fact built of wood recycled from sturdy whisky crates that served during the islands' notorious heyday as an *entrepôt* during the US Prohibition Era of the 1920s. The best known, on Savoyard Road, is named after a time-honoured brand, Cutty Sark Villa. Indeed, the town's most interesting cultural attraction is the Prohibition Exhibit of photographs and whisky-running artefacts in what was once the police barracks and is now the Hotel Roberts. The straw hat is said to have been left here during an inspection visit by Al Capone. A tribute to the Free French naval invasion in 1941—without a shot being fired in anger—comes almost as an afterthought.

The town museum traces the islands' history with models of the Basque, Norman and Breton sailing ships bringing fishermen here from the 16th century. French explorer Jacques Cartier claimed the territory for France in 1536 (16 years after its discovery by Portuguese navigator Alvarez Fagundes). The islands passed back and forth between the French and British until they became definitively French by the Treaty of Paris of 1815.

Pointe de Savoyard is the islanders' own resort area on the northwest coast, their pretty little summer cottages commanding a fine view of Petite-Miquelon. Windsurfers appreciate the ideal conditions of Savoyard Pond. Hunters cross over to Petite-Miquelon to stalk the Canadian white-tailed deer with which the stunted spruce forests have been stocked since the 1950s. Half-wild horses roam free on the Miquelons, descendants of survivors from shipwrecks.

The humpback whale takes a powerful leap into the air: a thrilling sight for whale-watchers.

For an overview of the town and the Bay of Islands, go up to the **Captain James Cook Monument**, a national historic site set up to display copies of charts drawn up by the explorer in 1764.

East of the town centre, on Farnell's Lane, visit the amazing **Sticks and Stones House**, open to the public since 1987. The owner of the house, Mr Farnell himself, spent 25 years of his life applying his very personal style of interior decorating to all his walls and ceilings, sticking ice-lolly sticks and various retrieved bits and pieces such as camera flashbulbs, buttons and pebbles in obsessive patterns.

On Station Road, you can look around relics of the narrow-gauge railway: the **Historic Train** comprises a gleaming locomotive, dining and sleeping cars and a

114

work train restored by the Newfoundland Railway Society.

In the town centre, the **Royal Newfoundland Constabulary Museum**, on University Drive, traces the history of the Newfie police. Relax in nearby **Margaret Bowater Park**, a wooded area with walking trails, river and waterfall, and picnic spots.

THE ISLAND'S OTHER RESIDENTS

Newfoundland's wildlife boasts some of nature's most majestic creatures. Some 40,000 woodland caribou roam the scarcely populated interior. The biggest of these larger North American versions of the reindeer can weigh up to 320 kg (705 lb) and sport fine antlers, both male and female. But the most magnificent antlers, flattened and wide spread, are sported by the island's 70,000 hump-backed moose. Weighing up to 540 kg (1,200 lb), they nonetheless move at remarkable speed over marshy terrain and negotiate a path through dense forest. Black bear are basically vegetarian, but not religiously so, eating anything and anyone to get up to their fighting weight of well over 300 kg (670 lb).

Every year, fly-rod fishermen thrill to the challenge of migratory Atlantic salmon when they make their spawning move up the clear unpolluted waters of the island's gravel-bedded rivers. These may be rushing torrents or babbling brooks. Inland, it changes from its ocean diet of crustaceans to small fish as reaches a weight of 7 kg (more than 15 lb). The landlocked Sebago salmon known locally as ouananiche is smaller but just as tasty, as are the rainbow trout—despite its name, more aggressive than the American cut-throat trout—and the mild-mannered speckled eastern brook trout.

Offshore, watching for the humpback whale is a favourite sport. Grey-black with whitish fins, it measures up to 15 m (50 ft) in length and weighs up to 40 tons. It can be as playful as a dolphin, and this is the one whose chirruping songs have often topped the hit-parade charts.

Frustrated American patriots may spot their national bird, the bald eagle—so rare back home—hovering above the island's fjords. In fact, it is not bald, just white-headed. Newfoundland's official bird is the Atlantic puffin, which can often be seen along the shore clutching a bunch of white bait in its red, blue and yellow beak. The quaint-looking green-headed merganser or goosander is dismissed by hunters as a "trash duck" due to the rank, fishy taste of its flesh.

Geology buffs should make an excursion to the forested hills of **Gros Morne National Park**; its Tablelands plateau is one of the world's best examples of rock heaved up from the earth's interior. This remarkable topography of flatlands enclosed by undulating hills is produced by what the scientists call continental drift. The high cliffs of the Long Range Mountains towering over the fjords are clad in the greenery of stunted pine woods and arctic-alpine plants. The wildlife here includes rock ptarmigan, arctic hare and caribou. The highest peak is Gros Morne itself, 806 m (2,643 ft). For one perspective on the natural wonders, take the boat trip around scenic **Bonne Bay**. At the northern end of the park, the sand dune beaches of **Shallow Bay** offer a haven of peace and quiet and even, in high summer, a refreshing dip in the sea.

The road north from St Paul's has been designated the Viking Trail, leading to **L'Anse aux Meadows National Historic Site**. A thousand years of history is preserved and honoured here, on the spot where Leif Eriksson founded a colony he called Vinland around AD 1000. Leif stayed a year before returning to Greenland. (During a later voyage to the same colony, the first European was born in the New World; his name was Snorri.)

It wasn't until 1960 that tenacious Norwegian archaeologists uncovered the ruins of Vinland, confirming the sagas of the Vikings settling North America. L'Anse aux Meadows is now a UNESCO World Heritage Site where you can see a re-creation of the original sod houses and hear the tales of the great adventure. Just south of the historical site is the charming little port town of **St Anthony**. On the west side of town, visit the museum at **Grenfell House**, home of an Englishman who came to Newfoundland in 1892 and founded the Grenfell hospital mission.

The **Strait of Belle Isle** separates Newfoundland from the mainland, with a ferry service linking it to Blanc Sablon on the Quebec-Labrador boundary, 18 km (11 miles) away. If you cross over in late spring or early summer, you will encounter melting icebergs carried from Greenland by the Labrador Current. They break up in the warmer waters of the St Lawrence.

Eating Out

Hearty is the word for local fare, featuring seafood, and lots of it. Fried cod tongues, similar to clams in taste and texture, rate as the great local delicacy.

In the range of unusual traditional dishes, there's "fish and brewis" (pronounced "brooz"), a

Newfoundland's tables positively groan beneath the weight of seafood.

stew of boiled salt cod and ship's biscuit, and "cod and scrunchions", boiled salt cod and crackling.

For a sweet, the locals favour "figged duff", old-fashioned raisin and molasses pudding, or a bowlful of the marsh, squash or partridge berries found only in this part of the world. Most popular of all are Arctic cloudberries. Known locally as "bakeapples", the soft orange berries do indeed taste like baked apple. Wash it all down with tea, rum (referred to as "screech" in Newfoundland) or the excellent Canadian beer.

Shopping

Knitwear. A cottage industry in Newfoundland. Shops in St John's and Corner Brook carry handknitted, embroidered and crocheted sweaters, scarves, gloves and hats.

Gemstones and jewellery. Look for labradorite, an attractive blue semi-precious stone. You can buy it in the rough, in a finished state, or worked into necklaces, cufflinks and other pieces.

Indian crafts. Carvings of Canadian birds and animals are offered for sale, along with articles of deer- and sealskin.

117

Specialities. Partridgeberry jam, sealmeat pie, cod tongues, potted moose and so on will surely intrigue your friends back home.

Woven goods. The choice ranges from scarves to place mats. Hooked rugs are another island speciality, with fishes and flowers worked into the pattern.

Practical Information

Banks. Generally open Monday to Friday 10 a.m. to 3 p.m. Some banks open on Saturdays.

Climate. Not as cold as you'd think. The temperature on the coast averages 20°C (68 °F) maximum in summer, –2 °C (29°F) maximum in winter.

Currency. The Canadian dollar is divided into 100 cents. Notes: $5 to $1,000. Coins: 1¢ to $2.

Telephone. Newfoundland (area code 709) is part of the US network. To call the UK, dial 011 44 then the area code minus the initial zero, and the local number.

Time. Newfoundland time is GMT –3$^1/_2$ (– 2$^1/_2$ in summer): half an hour ahead of Atlantic Standard Time and 1$^1/_2$ hours ahead of Eastern Standard Time.

New Brunswick

Gateway to Atlantic Canada

New Brunswick is the scene of much of Canada's early history in relation to Europe. The region was the object of recurring tugs-of-war between the French and the British until the mid-18th century, when England triumphed. After the American colonies won their independence (1783), thousands of diehard British Loyalists fled here. When the province was created, it was named after the German Duchy of Braunschweig, ruled by George III.

By the second half of the 19th century, the shipbuilding industry had made New Brunswick the most prosperous province in Canada; two enterprising brothers from Chatham founded the Cunard Line. But when steam and steel replaced sails and wooden hulls, shipbuilding was doomed and the province's fortunes waned.

Bordering Quebec to the north, and the US state of Maine on the west, New Brunswick is linked to Nova Scotia by the Isthmus of Chignecto and to Prince Edward Island by a toll bridge. It remains a dual-language province, with 35 per cent speaking French amidst an English-speaking majority. Most of the population lives along the river valleys and coastal strips and in the southeast lowlands; few inhabit the densely forested interior.

The Saint John River dominates the landscape, gliding through hilly, lush forests and undulating farmland, occasionally plunging in roiling cascades. Flowing past Fredericton, the leafy provincial capital, and gradually broadening, it culminates in the rugged port of Saint John.

A Brief History

Early times	New Brunswick is inhabited by the Micmac Indians.
16th–17th centuries	In 1534 Jacques Cartier explores Chaleur Bay off the north coast, and in 1604 Samuel de Champlain lands briefly at the mouth of the Saint John River, site of present-day Saint John. In 1631 Charles de la Tour builds a trading fort bearing his name at the river mouth, and in 1692, another is built upstream at Fredericton, soon to be abandoned.
18th–19th centuries	On the site of Fredericton's fort the settlement of Pointe-St-Anne takes root from 1732. The British gain control of New Brunswick in mid-18th century, expelling the French-speaking Acadians, many of whom head for Louisiana. In 1783–84 some 14,000 Loyalists arrive in New Brunswick,

turning Saint John and Fredericton into boom towns. At the same time, New Brunswick becomes a province separate from Nova Scotia. Fredericton is named provincial capital and a college (now university) founded. Saint John flourishes as a shipbuilding centre until timber is replaced by steel.

The frontier with the US state of Maine is set definitively by the Webster-Ashburton Treaty of 1842. In 1867 New Brunswick becomes part of the Canadian Confederation.

Sightseeing

Saint John

With 80,000 inhabitants, Saint John ranks as New Brunswick's biggest town. In its 19th-century heyday, it was called "the Liverpool of America", and even today it is an active port, open all year. While the traditional shipbuilding has diminished, modernization of the paper-and-pulp and fishing industries, along with tourism, has given the town a second wind.

As so many of Saint John's original inhabitants fled here after the American colonies won independence, it's not surprising that the town is known as "Loyalist City". You can't get away from these connections, highlighted in streets named Crown, Queen, King, Princess, Duke and others.

The downtown area juts out on a peninsula into the bay east of the Saint John River. The actual centre is **King Square**, an agreeable little park whose paths form the pattern of the Union Jack—another nod to the city's loyalties. The cheerful area harmoniously combines 19th- and 20th-century atmospheres, especially along red-brick King Street. **Old City Market**, Canada's oldest, makes an eye-catching sight off one corner of King Square with its stalls of seafood, vegetables and crafts.

East of the square lie the **Loyalist Burial Grounds** with tombstones dating from 1784. For walkers, there is a Loyalist Trail (brochure from the Visitors and Convention Centre), as well as a Victorian Stroll, playing up the buildings that replaced the many wooden ones destroyed in the fire of 1877. One remaining Georgian mansion, **Loyalist House** (1816), has been converted into a museum commemorating, you might have guessed, Loyalist history. Note the **Old Courthouse** of 1829, with the tall spiralling stone staircase, and the **Chubb Building**, where, in the late 18th century, Mr Chubb had all the town's

notables and his own children sculpted in rosettes on the façade of the building. One way of achieving immortality!

The Bay of Fundy's extraordinary tides are responsible for one of Saint John's main attractions, the **Reversing Falls** rapids. The best view of the phenomenon can be had from Reversing Falls Bridge. The effects of the tides can be felt right up to Fredericton, 130 km (80 miles) away.

The renovated harbourfront features **Market Square**, a delightful multi-level residential and commercial complex, replacing dreary warehouses. It was here at Market Slip that the famous contingent of Loyalists landed in 1783 and brought good times to the city. The event is given its rightful importance in mid-July by the Loyalist City Festival. A century later, thousands of Irish immigrants arrived at the same site. Many were quarantined on Canada's equivalent of Ellis Island, Partridge Island, where a museum tells their story. **New Brunswick Museum** concentrates on the former glories of the shipbuilding industry that brought Saint John considerable wealth.

Offering a panoramic view over the whole city and the Bay of Fundy is **Carleton Martello Tower**, dating from the War of 1812 between Britain and the US. With its old barracks and powder magazine spiffily restored, it has been declared a National Historic Site.

Fredericton

Like Saint John, gracious, elm-shaded Fredericton, upstream on the Saint John River, began life as a French settlement, blossoming into a real town with the arrival of the British Loyalists, who renamed it after one of George III's sons. When the province of New Brunswick was created, Fredericton was named capital, Saint John being considered vulnerable to attack by sea. Hence a good bulk of Fredericton's 50,000-strong population works for the provincial government.

The French-revival **Legislative Building** is its seat, a silver-domed sandstone structure built in 1880 to replace the former one destroyed by fire. Tourists can enter to admire the Assembly Chamber and its tiered balcony. A handsome wooden spiral staircase leads to the parliamentary library, which has one of the few copies extant of the *Domesday Book*, William the Conqueror's census of England, as well as a rare complete set of Audubon's *Birds of America*.

The Legislative Building dominates the north end of **The Green**, a strip of parkland stretching along the river, and the

123

Beaverbrook Art Gallery, one of the foremost art centres in the nation. It contains a wide collection of British masters—Gainsborough, Hogarth, Lawrence, Reynolds, Constable, Turner—although the continental section is also important. There is also a fine display of Canadian artists, and tapestries, porcelain, and furniture.

Neo-Gothic **Christ Church Cathedral**'s lofty spire rises south on The Green. Built in the 1880s, it was the first new cathedral erected on British soil since the Norman Conquest and patterned after a Norfolk parish church. Note the wooden hammer-beam ceiling.

North on the riverbank, set behind a black wrought-iron fence, the old **Military Compound** still maintains a symbolic martial presence. The Changing of the Guard takes place daily in Officers' Square in summer, provided the weather behaves itself.

The **York-Sunbury Historical Society Museum** is housed in old officers' quarters. Here you can glean a picture of the city over the centuries, with interesting displays on the first inhabitants, the Indians, and on life in a garrison town. Then you'll stumble on a little local lore in the museum's weirdest exhibit—the stuffed 19-kg (42-lb) Coleman Frog, squatting in all his gargantuan glory. The amphibian was adopted by a local and fattened up on rum pudding and June bugs in honey sauce!

Up the Saint John

Upstream near Fredericton is **Kings Landing Historical Settlement**. Typical buildings of the period 1783 to 1900 have been transplanted to the site in order to re-create a Loyalist village. The "inhabitants" in period dress go happily about their daily chores as in the past.

Further north near Hartland is the world's longest **covered bridge**, dating from 1899. With

---

THE BOUNTIFUL LORD

The Beaverbrook Art Gallery and a large part of its art collection were the gift of one William Maxwell Aitken, reared in Newcastle, New Brunswick, who left Canada for London to establish a press empire. Elevated to the peerage as Lord Beaverbrook, he became an influential figure in the World War II cabinet of Winston Churchill. Loyal to his home even thought he was absent from it most of his life, he financed myriad cultural institutions in New Brunswick. In Fredericton his largess extended also to The Playhouse theatre and several university buildings.

its seven spans, it is a picturesque, much-photographed sight.

Grand Falls (Grand-Sault), as its name implies, is the site of a thundering waterfall, where the Saint John River takes a dramatic 23-m (75-ft) plunge. The river proceeds to churn its way through a deep and narrow horseshoe-shaped gorge, scooping out circular potholes here and there. A hydro-electric power plant has been built to draw on the unleashed energy. A flight of stairs leads down to the gorge with its walking trails and several vantage points.

Other Provincial Highlights

The **Fundy Isles** in Passamaquoddy Bay near the border with Maine, site of Champlain's first settlement, are a popular resort area. On Campobello Island is Franklin Delano Roosevelt's 34-room cottage, preserved exactly as it was when the US president lived there.

Other touristic imperatives are the **Fundy National Park**, rolling parkland indented by deep valleys and fringed with tidal flats full of marine life; **The Rocks** at Hopewell Cape, bizarre sandstone formations carved out of the cliffs by wind and tide; and **Fort Beausejour**, built in 1713 by the French to thumb their noses at the British across the border in Nova Scotia.

Eating Out

The smartest thing to order in New Brunswick is lobster, at its best boiled or broiled, with melted butter and lemon as the only flavourings. The region is also justly proud of its broiled salmon and shad amandine. Other irresistible seafood are oysters, be they fresh, stewed or turned into a bisque; scallops, particularly delicious fried; clams turned into a chowder along with onions, potatoes and milk; or cod in myriad imaginative manifestations.

The province has one of Canada's largest potato crops, and they make an excellent accompaniment to fish or meat. Be adventurous and try the unusual steamed fiddlehead, an edible fern that is often served along with roast lamb.

For dessert, specialities of the region revolve around blueberries, rhubarb and strawberries.

Shopping

In Saint John, the Trinity Royal end of Prince William and Canterbury streets, with its unique boutiques, antiques and handicrafts, is *the* place to shop. In Fredericton, try Regent, Queen, York, King and the adjacent side streets, as well as Woodstock Road. You'll find any number of craft specialities, such as pewter, pottery, weaving, quilts, woodworking, stained glass, enamel jewellery… The art galleries will surely tempt you with their seascapes and coastal landscapes. Or you may want to bring back a few metres of the official New Brunswick tartan to stitch up into something novel.

For a souvenir truly "of the region"—synonymous with the great outdoors—a hunting jacket or parka couldn't be more practical. The ultimate item of clothing for shielding you from the elements would be a fisherman's oilskin or sou'wester hat.

Practical Information

Credit cards are widely accepted, as are traveller's cheques in Canadian or American currency

Currency. The Canadian dollar is divided into 100 cents. Notes: $5 to $1,000. Coins: 1¢ to $2.

Customs. New Brunswick's legal drinking age is 19. Liquor is sold in government stores.

Electricity. 110 volts, 60 cycles. European appliances will require a transformer and an adaptor.

Measures. Canada is on the metric system, with temperatures in Celsius and distances and speed limits in kilometres.

Taxes. Foreigners can request a cash rebate of the 7% Goods and Services Tax (GST) levied on their accommodations and the goods they will export.

Time. Atlantic Standard Time, or GMT – 4. Daylight Saving Time (when clocks advance one hour) is observed from the first Sunday in April to the last Sunday in October.

Tipping. Tips or services charges in hotels and restaurants are left to the client. A tip of 10–15% is customary, which also applies to barbers and hairdressers, taxi drivers. Porters and chambermaids will appreciate a small gratuity as well.

Transport. Free government-operated ferries provide service in the lower Saint John River area and to islands in the Bay of Fundy.

Nova Scotia

Scots-French Heritage

There's more than a touch of the Gaelic about Nova Scotia— "New Scotland" in Latin. Especially on Cape Breton Island, the northeastern outcrop of the Atlantic province, linked to the mainland by causeway. Scots were first given landrights in 1621, but they really arrived in force in the early 19th century—some 50,000 Scots highlanders flocked to the island, bringing their language, kilts, bagpipes, dances and even their place-names with them. Their descendants have kept this culture very much alive.

With its dramatic seascapes and rugged highlands, it's no surprise that Cape Breton is the province's foremost tourist venue. Although the island's capital Sydney is dominated by steel mills and coal mines, it makes a good base for the principal attractions round about: the spectacular Cabot Trail, the inland sea Bras d'Or… and the mighty French fortress of Louisbourg.

Indeed, there's no forgetting the French took root in Nova Scotia first. On the Bay of Fundy side of the peninsula proper, French history really comes alive along the Evangeline Trail, with Champlain's colony from 1605 and the French speaking Acadian villages of St Mary's Bay. Halifax itself, the provincial capital, was built as a British counterweight to the French presence at Louisbourg. With its superb harbour and strategic position, Halifax more than proved its worth to the British, in its campaign for Canada, during the American Revolution and again in the War of 1812. As the Atlantic base of the Canadian Navy, Halifax continues to play a major role in the country's defences. After visiting the citadel and historic sights, tourists should strike out west for the rugged coastline and pretty fishing villages of the Atlantic Shore. There are over 7,500 km (4,700 miles) of coastline all told in Nova Scotia.

A Brief History

11th century	Leif Erikson is thought to set foot on the coast of Nova Scotia about AD 1000. The land is inhabited by Micmac Indians.
15th–17th centuries	English navigators John and Sebastian Cabot stop briefly on the northern tip of Cape Breton Island in 1497, claiming the entire continent for the Crown. European expeditions sail here, attracted by the cod and fur trade with the Indians.

The French try to settle the region from as early as 1518. After noting the fine natural harbour of Halifax, French explorers Sieur de Monts and Samuel de Champlain establish the small colony of Port Royal (Annapolis Royal) in 1605. But Britain believes it has a prior claim to the region and the competition is on. In 1621 King James I grants the land to Sir William Alexander, a fellow Scot, on the condition that he creates a "New Scotland". Eleven years later, however, Charles I cedes the territory to the French.

18th century

The Treaty of Utrecht (1713) gives mainland Nova Scotia to the British, while Cape Breton Island remains with the French. The town of Halifax is founded in 1749 by Edward Cornwallis as a military and naval counterweight to the French fort on Cape Breton. It proves an invaluable base for the British conquest of Canada. In 1763 all French territory in Canada passes to Britain. Mistrusting the Acadian French, the British drive them from mainland Nova Scotia in 1755.

During the American Revolution, Halifax serves as British headquarters on the continent. After the war, 25,000 Loyalists from the colonies emigrate to Nova Scotia, where they establish shipbuilding industries.

19th century

Halifax again serves as an important base for the British in the War of 1812. Cape Breton Island is annexed to Nova Scotia in 1820. Nova Scotia joins the provinces of New Brunswick, Ontario and Quebec in forming the Confederation of Canada in 1867. Sydney experiences moderate growth, with the opening of coal mines and increasing use of the harbour.

20th century

Sydney's economy booms as its steel plant feeds Canada's great railway building programme in the years before World War I, but as the century progresses, the coal and steel industries decline. In compensation, Cape Breton becomes one of the prime tourist centres of eastern Canada. The war brings prosperity and growth to Halifax also, and its port continues vital for Canadian trade—it sees its busiest time in winter when the St Lawrence Seaway closes down.

Today, fishing is Nova Scotia's chief source of employment, while the economy is strongest in manufacturing, timber and engineering.

Sightseeing

Halifax

Halifax is an industrious, forward-looking city of more than 320,000, counted together with its twin city of Dartmouth across the inlet. It figures as the commercial, financial and educational centre of the Atlantic Provinces and one of the world's great ports. About three-quarters of the population are of English origin, one out of ten claims French descent, and Scottish, Irish, German and black groups complete the Haligonian ethnic mix.

High up on the hill dominating Halifax, the **Citadel** is the place where it all began. Edward Cornwallis, the town's founder, chose the site for its excellent defensive position and the sweeping view of the harbour and surrounding land. The town itself was laid out on the slope below, facing the harbour.

The present star-shaped fortress, the fourth on the spot, was built in 1829. The British were constantly improving the fortifications to keep them up to date and equal to the latest military developments. As you'll see, the **view** from the Citadel is something spectacular. There's an audio-visual show on the history of the fortress and the interesting **Army Museum**. You can tour the restored barracks, powder magazines and the maze-like corridors leading to defensive positions. Block your ears if you're there at noon. Every day at 12 sharp they fire off a cannon, a custom begun more than a century ago.

Directly below the Citadel, the **Old Town Clock** (1803) has become the symbol of Halifax. Edward, Duke of Kent, Commander-in-Chief of Nova Scotia and father of Queen Victoria, had the clock designed by his own engineers and presented it to the city.

Grand Parade Square, part of the original city plan, started off as a place of assembly and drill-ground for the local militia. At one end is **St Paul's** (1750), the oldest Protestant church in the country and the oldest building in Halifax. Its cemetery, the **Old Burying Ground** three blocks to the south, contains the graves of many of the town's original settlers. Other Halifax churches of note are the **Old Dutch Church** in Brunswick Street, only 12.5 m long by 6 m wide (40 ft x 20 ft), built by German settlers (*Deutsch* called *Dutch* in the local parlance) in 1856, and **St George's**, also in Brunswick Street, an unusual ecclesiastical phenomenon: a round church.

Two handsome government buildings remain from the Georgian period. You can tour **Province House** (1818), Canada's old-

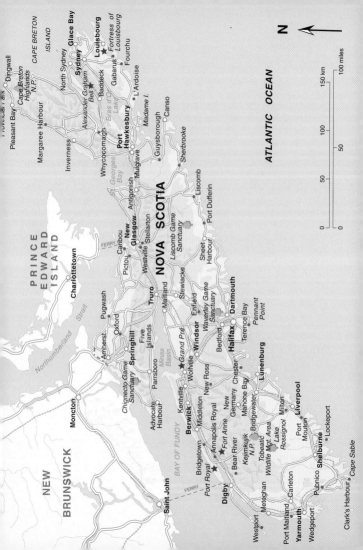

est parliamentary hall, with its fine collection of portraits of the British royal family. Charles Dickens proclaimed it "a gem of Georgian architecture". Across from Province House is the **Art Gallery of Nova Scotia**, integrating modern gallery facilities in a renovated heritage building. It houses the finest art collection in eastern Canada.

Over by the harbour you'll find the **Historic Properties**, Halifax's bright and breezy waterfront redevelopment project. Old warehouses, once used by privateers to store their booty, have been transformed into craft and specialty shops, restaurants and pubs. It's attractively done and very popular with both Haligonians and visitors. In the same complex is the **Maritime Museum of the Atlantic**, devoted to the city's long involvement with the sea, and **Summit Place**, the tall glass building that hosted the G-7 meetings of world leaders in 1995.

The **Brewery Market Complex** nearby is the site of an animated weekend farmers' market, where you can pick up some of the celebrated Nova Scotia salmon. If you were looking forward to gorging yourself on smoked salmon, you're in for a big disappointment. It's a luxury item

---

THE HALIFAX EXPLOSION

In the north of Halifax, in the centre of a park, stands a starkly jagged metallic memorial to the victims of a terrible calamity that befell the port on December 6, 1917. A French munitions ship, the *Mont Blanc*, loaded with 25,000 tons of explosives, collided with a Norwegian vessel, provoking the largest man-made detonation ever experienced before the atom bomb.

The blast was seen and heard over 100 km (60 miles) away and turned the northern part of the city into what was described as "a vast burning scrapyard, over which hung an enormous billowing cloud". Official figures showed that 1,963 died, 9,000 were injured and 199 blinded. And more than 25,000 Haligonians were left homeless in the bitter cold.

The *Mont Blanc*'s anchor landed 3 km (2 miles) away from where the ship exploded—and there it still lies, on the far side of the North West Arm. Other evidence of the explosion can be seen at St Paul's Church; preserved by double glazing since the time of the blast is the hole blown in one of the windows—the distinct shape of a man's profile.

here, too, because salmon fishing has been severely restricted around Nova Scotia for reasons of conservation.

At Privateer's Wharf behind Historic Properties, look for **Bluenose II**, a replica of the famous racing schooner pictured on the Canadian dime. *Bluenose I* was the undefeated champion of the North American fishing fleet for 25 years. Bluenoses, by the way, are Nova Scotians, who endure the province's rugged climate and perhaps have blue noses to show for it.

A **cruise** on the *Bluenose II* (or one of the other boat tours leaving from Privateer's Wharf) is an excellent way to see the harbour. 133

ACADIAN EXODUS

Sorrow and silence are strong,
and patient endurance is godlike.
Henry Wadsworth Longfellow

These words from Longfellow's poem *Evangeline* sum up the sad tale of the exile of "Acadia's" French settlers.

To the French, who were there first, Nova Scotia was always Acadie. (They mistook *ak-a-de*, which appeared at the end of many Indian place-names, for the name of the country, though in fact it meant "place of".)

The French founded Port Royal (Annapolis) in 1605 and turned to farming the fertile Annapolis Valley. But British ambitions in the area led to a bloody conflict for supremacy. After several attempts by a determined and far superior force of New Englanders to gain control, the French were finally subdued, and in 1713 the Treaty of Utrecht ceded mainland Nova Scotia to the British.

A generation of peace allowed the Acadian farmers to prosper—until relations between France and Britain deteriorated again. The Acadians were immediately suspected as subversives and given an ultimatum: take an oath of allegiance or face exile. The Acadians refused, knowing full well that the oath would mean military service against France.

On September 5, 1755, at the Church of St Charles, the Acadians heard the fatal words: "That your lands and tenements, cattle of all kinds and livestock of all sorts, are forfeited to the Crown, and you yourself to be removed from this… Province".

More than 10,000 were forcibly deported, mostly to the American Colonies, some to France and others to the Magdalen Islands. Those that ended up in Louisiana became known as *Cajuns*, derived from *Acadiens* and still in use. Families and friends were often brutally separated, a situation that provided Longfellow with his theme for *Evangeline*.

Barely two decades later, a few exiles returned. They found their homes and lands in the Annapolis Valley had been appropriated by the New Englanders, but they marched bravely through and on to St Mary's Bay, where they settled and turned their talents to fishing. And there they still are, their neat little villages lining the coastal road.

Some of the two-hour cruises take in the shipyards and dockyards and then sail down past lovely **Point Pleasant Park**, the **Martello Tower** built by the Duke of Kent to guard the harbour entrance, and over into **Northwest Arm**, a delightful inlet lined with vacation homes and boating and bathing clubs.

The **Nova Scotia Museum of Natural History** on Summer Street behind the Citadel will tell you all about the people of the region and the land they live on. The exhibits include a number of model houses from earlier days.

Farther down on Summer Street are Halifax's beautiful **Public Gardens**, 7 ha (18 acres) of trees, flowers, ponds and fountains. In summer, they hold concerts here in a bandstand built for Queen Victoria's Jubilee.

York Redoubt, south of the city, also played a part in Halifax's defences. The Duke of Kent built it over earlier fortifications high up on a bluff overlooking the harbour. The tower was still in use as a command post in World War II.

A popular excursion from Halifax goes to **Peggy's Cove**, a picturesque fishing village southeast of town. Photographers just can't resist the sight of the peaceful harbour surrounded by impressive granite boulders where the waves come crashing in. Priva-

teers also favoured the rugged coast around Peggy's Cove and rumours abound of treasure buried here.

Annapolis Royal

In 1605, after barely surviving the winter on St Croix Island (New Brunswick) because of scanty food supplies, French explorer Samuel de Champlain gave up his settlement there as a bad idea and moved across the Bay of Fundy to establish a fur-trading post at **Port Royal Habitation**, near present-day Annapolis Royal. The new colony had little more success, lasting only eight years until it was destroyed by a force of Virginians. Today it has been re-created using Champlain's original sketches and authentic 17th-century construction techniques. You'll find a governor's house, guard room, priest's house, bakery, blacksmith's shop and several other buildings, all surrounded by a palisade fence.

When the Habitation was lost, the French founded a new settlement nearby. That, too, was captured in 1710 by the British, who renamed the moated stronghold **Fort Anne** and the colony Annapolis Royal, after their queen. The town served as Nova Scotia's first capital until 1749, when Halifax assumed the honour. Fort Anne, like the Habitation, is now

a national historic site, with its well-kept grassy lawns belying a battle-scarred past. A small museum highlights the repeated struggles between the French and the British.

Nearby, don't miss the beautiful **Historic Gardens**, and take the time to seek out the several dwellings of historic value, including the De Gannes-Cosby House, the oldest wooden house in Canada.

The **Annapolis Valley**, called the Evangeline Trail (see p. 134), winds its way through rich farmland and fruit orchards and is especially delightful to drive through in late May to early June,

when it sparkles with white apple blossoms. Magnificent 18th- and 19th-century homes of sea captains and planters dot the way. If you make the whole journey, you'll be rewarded with a spectacular **panorama** over the Valley and the Minas Basin from the Lookoff on Route 358, and at trail's end, gaze on the breathtaking cliffs of **Cape Split**.

Sydney

Lying on the edge of a huge coalfield, Sydney makes no claims to being a tourist attraction in itself. Its fortune has been built around coal and steel—traditional industries which have suffered badly in our time. But this 200-year-old city, population over 26,000, does offer the visitor some rare historical insights, as well as providing a base for sightseeing elsewhere on Cape Breton Island.

In Sydney you can see such gems as **St Patrick's Museum**, a restoration of the oldest standing Catholic church on Cape Breton Island; **Jost House** on Charlotte Street, the 200-year-old wooden home of a prominent merchant; and **Cossit House**, built for the rector of St George's in 1787 from lumber hauled from Virginia at a cost of $1,000. Nearby **St George's**, originally designed as a chapel for the British garrison, has served the Anglican community for 200 years. Its bell was made from a cannon recovered from the Crimean War. A great treasure kept within the altar rail is a Chippendale chair donated by the officers of Lord Nelson's flagship, the *Victory*.

The **Lyceum** on George Street was built in 1906 as a cultural and entertainment centre. Used now as an arts and crafts complex, it also offers live theatre, a museum of industrial life and a "Days-Gone-By Antique and Collectable Emporium".

In contrast to Gaelic culture, attempts are being made to preserve the lifestyle of the original inhabitants of Cape Breton—the Micmac Indians—at the **Meber-tou Reserve**, which is the only reserve in Canada located within city limits.

East of Sydney

The first sightseeing imperative out of Sydney is a visit to **Fortress Louisbourg**, just 37 km (23 miles) southeast. The original fortress, built by the French between 1720 and 1745, served briefly as the major fortification in Acadia, until its capture and demolition by the British. It lay in ruins for 200 years. Today, in what is acknowledged as the most ambitious restoration project ever undertaken in Canada, much of the fortress has been rebuilt. It is manned by mock soldiers and civilians in period dress, recreating the lifestyle of the mid-18th century. The bakery sells the kind of bread that the soldiers ate over 200 years ago, and in the Hôtel de la Marine, you can partake of an 18th-century meal, served in pewter dishes. The military quarters in the King's Bastion are of special interest: the ten elegant rooms of the Governor's Apartment are luxuriously furnished; the Officer's Quarters are more modest but still comfortable; the straw-strewn Soldier's Barracks are frankly stark and uninviting, and the "soldiers" shamelessly cultivate their slovenly appearance for the sake of authenticity.

137

Two hundred years of mining history is faithfully represented at the **Miners' Museum** in Glace Bay, northeast of Sydney. Here the ritual tour, with a veteran miner as escort, includes the Ocean Deeps Colliery shelving away under the sea. Nearby is the **Miner's Village**, portraying the home lives of these early pioneers, complete with restaurant lit by old mining lamps. A much-travelled miners' choir, known as the Men of the Deeps, gives weekly concerts to keep the old pit songs alive.

Also at Glace Bay, the **Marconi National Historic Site** documents the Italian inventor's telegraphic achievements in Cape Breton. Exhibits include a model of Marconi's original wireless radio station at Table Head, from which the first transatlantic message was sent in 1902 using electromagnetic waves instead of wires.

Cabot Trail

The 300-km (187-mile) Cabot Trail passes over mountains and through valleys, round the tip of

Cape Breton Island. It affords a unique opportunity to comprehend the diversity and beauty of the region. At a pinch, you can do the trip in a day, but it's best not to rush it. The scenery is wonderful in autumn, when the leaves turn every shade of gold and red.

Baddeck, 80 km (48 miles) from Sydney, on the northern shore of **Bras d'Or lake**, is generally considered the starting point of the circular trail. The town was chosen by Alexander Graham Bell, inventor of the telephone, for his summer home, which he named Beinn Bhreagh ("beautiful mountain" in Gaelic). Many of the inventor's wide interests are represented in the tetrahedron-shaped **Alexander Graham Bell Museum**. Apart from early models of the telephone, you can see some strange devices for making drinking water from fog, breath or salt water, and examples of Bell's researches in the aeronautical field. A prize exhibit is the replica of his hydrofoil (HD-4) which, powered by two aircraft engines, notched up a speed of more than 112 kph (70 mph) on Bras d'Or lake in 1919.

Following the trail in a clockwise direction, you reach North East Margaree, a small town with two unusual museums. The **Cape Breton Heritage Museum** illustrates the diverse cultures of the islanders, with the handicrafts of the Micmac Indians, Acadian French and Highland Scots, in particular a magnificent collection of tartans. In the **Salmon Museum** you can see the whole life cycle of the Atlantic salmon, from the egg to the adult's return up-river to reproduce.

The **Margaree Valley** is renowned for its salmon fishing. It leads to the west coast, which is dotted with little fishing villages where French is spoken. **Cheticamp** is especially famed for the hooked rugs made there. Occasionally, this art is demonstrated by experts in the **Acadian Museum**.

A few miles north of Cheticamp, the road enters the **Cape Breton Highlands National Park**. The scenery is magnificent; one minute you're in a green valley, the next you can see the sea pounding against the rugged rocky shores. At Pleasant Bay the road turns inland, cutting off the tip of the peninsula. A curiosity not to be missed along the route is **Lone Shieling**, the nostalgic replica of a highland crofter's cottage, complete with thatched roof. The trail follows the North Aspy River towards the village of **Cape North** on the east coast, where the villagers have Scots accents and Gaelic names. From here you can make a detour to the small fishing community of Bay

St Lawrence, 16 km (10 miles) to the north. The road passes through **Sugarloaf**, the place where Cabot is said to have landed in 1497.

Sandy beaches, hidden bays and coves, pink rocks and cliffs line the coast down to all the **Ingonishes**—Ingonish Centre, Ingonish Beach, Ingonish Harbour, Ingonish Island and just plain Ingonish. Together they form a popular resort with many sporting facilities, including skiing in winter.

A little further on, from Jersey Cove just south of Indian Brook, you can take a ferry across St Ann's Bay to **Englishtown**, which boasts the grave of Angus MacAskill, the local giant. Angus died in 1863, at the respectable height of 236 cm (7 ft 9 in). His possessions are on display in the

Giant MacAskill Museum. The local hero toured the United States with the celebrated midget General Tom Thumb.

From Englishtown you can drive straight on to Sydney, or you can return to the Cabot Trail and visit the **Gaelic College of Celtic Arts and Crafts** at St Ann's, a repository of the history and culture of the Scots. Each August this unique college admits visitors to student bagpipes-and-drums performances and stages a week-long Gaelic Mod.

Further south, another shop-window for the Gaelic is the **Nova Scotia Highland Village** at Iona, overlooking the Bras d'Or. It features a group of refurbished buildings, including a forge, carding mill, school and cabin, re-flecting the lifestyle of early Scots settlers.

Eating Out

Nova Scotia has a hearty cuisine, which may have something to do with the gourmet feasts organized by Samuel de Champlain at Port Royal to kill time in the long winters.

Acadian cooking is renowned for such traditional dishes as rapie pie, which combines clams or chicken with grated potatoes, and *fricot*, a soup of chicken, onions and potatoes that is substantial enough for a meal. Get your fill of the wonderful seafood dishes, such as steamed lobster, clam chowder, Digby scallops, smoked herring pâté and Solomon Gundy, a pickled herring recipe brought over by the Scots. Salmon may be expensive, but it is worth a splurge now and then, wonderful whether it is smoked and finely sliced, or cooked in the way of the Micmac Indians, on a plank before a roaring fire.

The lamb of Pictou County is renowned for its succulence, and Lunenburg, true to its German heritage, serves up delicious sausages, accompanied by potato salad spiked with apples, onions, and chives.

Desserts are of let's-not-count-the-calories richness, varying from spongecake trifles laced with raspberry jam and sherry to blueberry grunt. Local wines and beers are popular, but you need to be at least 19 to drink.

Shopping

Nova Scotia is the place to be for traditional Scots wear—princi-pally woollens and tartans. No less than 150 tartans are available at the store attached to the Gaelic College in St Ann's on Cape Breton Island. Superb hooked rugs are sold in some of the island's west coast villages, notably Che-ticamp. There are also more portable hookwork items, such as coasters, table mats and wall hangings.

The province has a wealth of handicrafts all out of proportion to its small size. Look also for hand-stitched quilts, red-clay pottery, hand-blown glass, pewter, gold and silver jewellery, leatherwork, Micmac quillwork, knitted items galore. Keep an eye out in antique shops for handwoven country baskets and eel traps.

Practical Information

Credit cards are widely accepted, as are traveller's cheques in Canadian or American currency.

Currency. The Canadian dollar is divided into 100 cents. Notes: $5 to $1,000. Coins: 1¢ to $2.

Customs. Nova Scotia's legal drinking age is 19. Liquor is sold in government stores. Restaurants that serve spirits are advertised as "licensed".

Electricity. 110 volts, 60 cycles. European appliances will require a transformer and an adapter.

Measures. Canada is on the metric system, with temperatures in Celsius and distances and speed limits in kilometres.

Taxes. Foreigners can request a cash rebate of the 7% Goods and Services Tax (GST) levied on their accommodations and the goods they will export.

Time. Atlantic Standard Time, or GMT – 4. Daylight Saving Time (when clocks advance one hour) is observed from the first Sunday in April to the last Sunday in October.

Tipping. Tips or services charges in hotels and restaurants are left to the client. A tip of 10–15% is customary, which also applies to barbers and hairdressers, taxi drivers. Porters and chambermaids will appreciate a small gratuity as well.

Transport. Ferry service connects Yarmouth with Bar Harbor and Portland, Maine; and Digby with Saint John, New Brunswick.

Prince Edward Island

Garden of the Gulf

Prince Edward Island, the land of *Anne of Green Gables*, will not disappoint you. It has remained a remarkably peaceful backwater—not very different from the place in the novel—with rolling green fields, tidy farms, terracotta cliffs, neat fishing villages, miles and miles of sandy beaches and blue waters.

Canada's smallest province, Prince Edward Island (PEI) is 225 km (140 miles) long and from 6 to 64 km (4 to 40 miles) wide. It nestles snugly in the Gulf of St Lawrence between New Brunswick and Nova Scotia. Because Nova Scotia shields it from the worst of the Atlantic weather, PEI enjoys more sunny days than its neighbours. About 130,000 people live on the island, 80 per cent of British descent, 17 per cent Acadian, 1 per cent Dutch and less than 1 per cent Micmac Indian.

More than three-quarters of the fertile island is under cultivation, giving rise to PEI's designation as the Garden of the Gulf. Potatoes are the main crop here, though they also raise blueberries, strawberries, tobacco and livestock. Fishing, too, is important, especially for lobster, cod and the excellent Malpeque oysters. But it's tourism that rates as the number two industry, with over half a million visitors each year. The superb beaches of the north shore boast amazingly warm water, 22°C (72°F) in summer—by far the balmiest bathing around. That and the 800 km (500 miles) of sandy shore explain PEI's popularity as a vacation site.

The Micmac Indians used to come here in summer, too. The fishing was good and the living was easy. Jacques Cartier's visit in 1534 had no immediate repercussions, since the French waited for another 186 years to found a colony on Ile Saint-Jean, as they called it. But of course, once the French arrived, the English became interested. They conquered the island in 1758, cleared out most of the French inhabitants, replacing them with American Loyalists and European immigrants. Many of today's islanders claim descent from 800 Scottish pioneers brought over in 1803 by the Earl of Selkirk.

Charlottetown, the capital—and only city—of PEI, is perfectly consistent with the low-key charm of the island. Named after the wife of George III, the town offers lots of greenery, native redstone buildings and Victorian gingerbread architecture. It's a busy port, a commercial and tourist centre, but Charlottetown all the same retains an old-fashioned air. In summer, they stage a festival here featuring concerts, plays and art exhibitions. And year in, year out, the most popular attraction is always the same: a musical version of *Anne of Green Gables*.

Charlottetown's big moment came in 1864 when the Fathers of the Confederation met here to talk about the formation of a Canadian nation. And though the city is still referred to as the birth-place of Canada, the proud and independent-minded islanders did not join the Confederation in 1867. It took them another six years to come round. As the Governor General of the country remarked, even then it seemed that they were under the impression that it was the Dominion of Canada that had been annexed to Prince Edward Island.

A Brief History

Early times — The Micmac Indians call the island Abegweit, "home cradled on the waves".

16th century — Jacques Cartier discovers the island in 1534, reporting it is "the fairest land 'tis possible to see". He promptly claims it for France, but the French make no move to settle the island, and the years pass without European colonization.

18th century — The French lose mainland Nova Scotia and decide to erect a fortress on Ile Saint-Jean, as they call the island, in 1720. They found Port La Joye (across the harbour from present-day Charlottetown), bringing in about 300 settlers The colony does not prosper, however, and famine finishes it off within 20 years. Acadian refugees from Nova Scotia arrive to make their home on the island.

The British take over Ile Saint-Jean in 1758 and its name becomes St John's. They deport the French inhabitants—all but 30 families, the ancestors of today's Acadians, who flee to the woods—and encourage settlers more sympathetic to Britain. The land is shared into 67 lots of 20,000 acres each, distributed through a lottery held in London: much of the island is thus owned by absentee landlords. St John's is annexed to Nova Scotia, and Charlottetown becomes the capital. Then St John's is separated from Nova Scotia. Yankee pirates pillage Charlottetown in 1775, carrying off the acting governor and several other officials to Massachusetts. The island is renamed in 1799 in honour of Prince Edward, Duke of Kent, Commander-in-Chief of Nova Scotia and father of Queen Victoria.

| 19th century | Originally heavily wooded, with timber its main resource, the island is gradually stripped of trees. Agriculture and shipbuilding become the mainstay of the economy. The population grows very slowly. The largest single group comes from Scotland in 1803. Many of today's islanders are descendants of these 800 Highlanders.

The Land Purchase Act of 1853 enables the government to buy back the land lots for resale to tenants. In 1864 a group of leaders from the eastern provinces, the Fathers of the Confederation, meet in Charlottetown to discuss the possibility of forming a Dominion of Canada. In 1967, Nova Scotia, New Brunswick, Quebec and Ontario join this new union; Prince Edward Island holds off until 1873. |
|---|---|
| 20th century | In recent years, Prince Edward Island has undergone the usual modernization and greatly developed its tourist facilities. But in appearance and outlook, the island remains steadfastly rural and faithful to its traditions. In 1997 the island is linked by a 13-km (8-mile) multi-span toll bridge from Borden to the New Brunswick mainland at Cape Tormentine. |

Sightseeing

Charlottetown

The two most important sights in Charlottetown stand close together in the centre of the city on Confederation Plaza. **Province House** is the sober, grey sandstone building in Georgian style. Completed in 1847, it served as the seat of the colonial government and now houses the Provincial Legislature. But Province House earned its place in Canadian history because it was chosen as the meeting place of the Fathers of the Confederation in 1864. Confederation Chamber has been kept exactly as it was on that historic occasion; you'll see the names of the participants alongside their chairs.

Next door stands the **Confederation Centre of the Arts**, opened in 1964 to commemorate the 100th anniversary of the Confederation Conference. All the provinces of Canada contributed to the costs of construction and now share in maintaining the centre. The many-faceted complex includes two theatres, a library, a museum and two art galleries, with a permanent collection of works by Canadian artists including several paintings by Robert Harris. It is also the home of the Charlottetown Summer Festival.

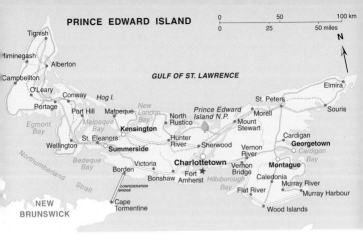

Across the street, **Hughes Drug Store** claims to be the oldest operating pharmacy in Canada. Many of the original fittings are still in place, along with the ornate woodwork.

With its twin Gothic-style spires, **St Dunstan's Basilica** (45 Great George Street) is an easily spotted city landmark. Inside, a beautiful rose window from Munich casts a soft light on the marble altar.

Take Queen Street up to City Hall, a neo-Romanesque structure of brick, and turn left into Kent. Here you'll see **Beaconsfield**, a gracious 25-room Victorian mansion built in 1877 by a wealthy ship merchant. Two floors, furnished in the Edwardian style, are open to the public.

Another fine building a few streets on is **Government House** (1834), the official residence of the Lieutenant Governor of PEI. It commands a splendid site overlooking the harbour with Victoria Park all around. Fort Edwards—now reduced to six cannons—is in the park, too.

Down by the waterfront, **Peake's Wharf** has been developed with restaurants and craft shops. You can take harbour tours from here. Across the harbour at **Rocky Point** are the remains of the island's first fortress, Port la Joye, put up by the French in 1720, and of Fort Amherst, the British installation of 1758. All that remains are some earthworks. For those lacking in imagination, an audio-visual presentation recreates the atmosphere of the place.

Reaching back even further in history is a replica of a **Micmac Village** where visitors can follow trails and seen how the Micmacs lived before the Europeans arrived. Indian handicrafts are on sale.

Around the Island

The Department of Tourism has marked out three scenic circuits of PEI, each well endowed with historical, cultural and recreational attractions.

Lady Slipper Drive, named after the provincial flower, covers 288 km (179 miles). It goes around the western third of the island, where the Acadian community lives. You'll find an Acadian Pioneer Village at Mont-Carmel and the Acadian Museum in Miscouche. The Green Park Shipbuilding Museum in Port Hill features the restored 19th-century shipyard and house that belonged to one James Yeo, Jr. The celebrated Malpeque oysters come from Malpeque Bay. On Lennox Island is a Micmac Reserve, with more than 50 families who are descendants of PEI's original inhabitants.

Kings Byway Drive traverses in 375 km (233 miles) the eastern end of the island, passing pleasant beaches, capes, covers, fishing ports, forest and farms. The Lord Selkirk Pioneer Settlement at Eldon contains some of the original log cabins built in the early 1800s by Scottish settlers. North Lake is a tuna fishing centre; Basin Head has an interesting Fisheries Museum.

The shortest and most convenient circuit from Charlottetown, **Blue Heron Drive**, still covers 190 km (120 miles), but of course, it's possible to do only a portion of the tour. Regular bus excursions from Charlottetown concentrate on the north shore. **PEI National Park** boasts some of the best beaches in Canada, in a setting of barrier islands, windswept dunes, red cliffs and salt marshes. A terrible gale raged

---

WILDLIFE

PEI birdwatchers can hardly miss the Great Blue Heron. This long-necked wader is a common sight around the island in many bays and inlets, digging for clams or taking off in a triumphal flutter of its powerful wings. It's one of more than 300 species of bird that visit PEI.

At the eastern end of the island, seal watching is a popular spectator sport. The sails hang out on the rocks, on sandbars and just swimming. Like the herons, they are connoisseurs of the local clams.

PEI National Park preserves miles of savagely beautiful coast.

off these shores in 1851, sinking 70 ships with a loss of 160 lives. The graves of many New England fishermen who drowned in that storm lie in a burial ground within the park.

Perhaps the single most popular attraction of the whole island, also part of the park, is **Green Gables House**, a neat white-frame farmhouse with green shutters and roof. Lucy Maud Mont- gomery spent many happy hours here as child and later used it as the setting for her novel. Green Gables fans can also visit the author's birthplace (New London); the Green Gables Post Office (Cavendish); Anne's House of Dreams (French River), a recreation of the fictional home of Anne and her new husband; and the Anne of Green Gables Museum at Silverbush.

149

Shopping

Island handicrafts make memorable souvenirs: paintings, knitwear, quilts, hooked rugs, ceramics, toys and dolls, jewellery. And everything connected with Anne, from books and videos to dolls and the inevitable Green Gables T-shirts.

Eating Out

Delicious, reasonably priced seafood is the big attraction here. Lobster is the centrepiece of meals that include salads, chowder mussels and the island's famous new potations. For further details, visit the Potato Museum in O'Leary.

Practical Information

Currency. The Canadian dollar is divided into 100 cents. US dollars are widely accepted for purchases; to change large sums go to the bank.

Tax refund. Non-residents of Canada can claim a refund for the 7 per cent Goods and Services Tax (GST). Rebate forms are available at tourist information centres.

Time difference. PEI keeps Atlantic Time (GMT –4), which is one hour later than Eastern Time.

General editor: Barbara Ender-Jones
English adaptation (Quebec): Judith Farr
Design: Luc Malherbe
Photos: Claude-Hervé Bazin; p. 8 Bernard Joliat; pp. 59, 84 Dominique Michellod;
p. 71 Erling Mandelmann; p. 86 Marinette Wannaz; pp. 95, 99, 100 Michael
Hockney; pp. 103, 110, 114, 117 Newfoundland Department of Tourism;
p. 119 Andrew Danson; pp. 127, 133, 136 Key-Colors/S. HINES;
pp. 138, 140 Spectrum Colour Library; pp. 143, 149 Maximilian Bruggmann;
Maps: Elsner & Schichor; p. 6–7, JPM Publications

Copyright © 1997/98 by JPM Publications S.A.
12, avenue William-Fraisse, 1006 Lausanne, Switzerland
All rights reserved. No part of this book may be reproduced or transmitted in any form or by any means, electronic or mechanical, including photocopying, recording or by any information storage and retrieval system without permission in writing from the publisher.
Every care has been taken to verify the information in the guide, but the publisher cannot accept responsibility for any errors that may have occurred. If you spot an inaccuracy or a serious omission, please let us know. Printed in Switzerland—Gessler

INDEX

151